@

## @AARLisa: New Biz i.

# Nuggets of Knowledge for Prospecting and Pitching smAARter

## Lisa Colantuono

**Praise For @AARLisa: New Biz in 140 Characters (or Less).**

"Lisa is a passionate industry advocate and an acknowledged agency search SME. Her innovative curation of agency selection-new business burning issues is timely, relevant and fascinating – a must read."

> **- Tom Finneran, EVP, Agency Management Services, American Association of Advertising Agencies**

"The big-picture-macro-view of the ever-shifting landscape of pitching marketing business in the consumer-driven-fragments digital age...in 140 characters. Love it!"

> **- Gregg Wasiak, Owner & Managing Partner, The Concept Farm**

"I find Lisa's quotes invaluable and inspirational – and because we're always pitching for new business, her 140 character or less gems are always relevant. On Twitter you rarely go back through Tweets and enjoy them – largely because you often Tweet from your phone. This book of Lisa's Tweets that you could thumb through and reference before, during or after new business, or just on a Sunday on the couch – is amazing."

> **- Noel Cottrell, EVP, Chief Creative Officer, Fitzgerald + Co.**

"Lisa's Tweet-like book of new business insights is genius, especially in this attention-deficit world. Wish I would have thought of it."

> **- Chris Shumaker, Chief Marketing Officer, FCB**

"Lisa's expertise in the marketing space, specifically as it relates to the delicate art of helping brands forge meaningful relationships with agencies, is just incomparable. The only thing that matches Lisa's remarkable depth of experience in aligning brands with agencies is her uncanny ability to share her very best practices through succinct yet actionable pearls of wisdom. Simply put, Lisa is a rare master at what she does and her operating principles deeply resonate with marketing professionals of all kinds through this book."

**- Simon Bond, Global Chief Growth Officer, IPG**

"When I read the New Business Tweets from Lisa, some themes become crystal clear to me. The new business process and winning pitches are all about integrity, chemistry, passion, people and most of all, common sense! The advice that Lisa gives is focused and consistent – extremely helpful to new business professionals who have to manage a lot of details, as well as all the people and personalities involved. Love the book! New business people are too busy to read anything BUT 140 character advice."

**- Barbara Stefanis-Israel, SVP, Director of Marketing, MARC USA**

"New business people are juggling 800 balls at any given moment, so bite-sized bits of info are a perfect way to communicate with us. Lisa's Tweets over the years have been insightful and extremely helpful in pitching and winning. @AARLisa: New Biz in 140 Characters (or Less) should be on the shelf of every agency person involved in the new business game."

**- Stephanie Sumner, VP Director, Business Development, McKinney**

"One line can win a pitch. Even after all the work an agency puts in, it really can come down to one line. That one line that sums everything up, that one line that lets a client see the future of their brand, or that one line that makes a connection between client and agency can make or break everything. In this book one of the business' leading search consultants, the lovely Lisa Colantuono, shares some one-liners (in 140 characters or less) that can help guide any agency to victory. Insightful, digestible, and fun – this book should be in the hands of every agency's new business lead and larger new business team."

- **Mike Ridley, Director of New Business,
the community**

"The advertising pitch business moves at 500 mph, with everyone excited and short of breath. What better way to witness that world than with the advice of a pitch expert in 140 characters or less! "

- **Bill Oberlander, Partner, Executive Creative Director,
Oberland**

"With Lisa's experience in new business, she's seen it all – the good, the bad and the ugly. If you're charged with running and growing an agency, the stories and lessons in this book should occupy an important place on your desk. We can always be better, and Lisa and this book can help us get there."

- **Matt Williams, CEO, The Martin Agency**

"You could write a book about all the advice people give you on new business prospecting. But who would read it? And if you did, you'd only remember the insights. Lisa has a cut-to-the-chase, highlights package of wisdom in today's new form of epithet...

the Tweet. Her knowledge and insight into this black art of commerce is voluminous in its brilliance and its brevity."

**- Sean Cummins, Global CEO, Cummins + Partners**

"Few people understand the function of new business at ad agencies with the amount of depth and insight that Lisa does. As anyone who follows her on Twitter knows, Lisa is passionate about sharing her knowledge so that agencies can get better at attracting and winning the right clients. You'd be hard-pressed to find a better advocate for both agencies and the marketers they serve."

**- Jody Sutter, Owner, The Sutter Company**

"In the world of new business for agencies, there are a handful of people who can provide practical, thoughtful advice on prospecting, pitching and performance management. Lisa Colantuono is one of those individuals who offer the wisdom of experience and the insights from observing agencies and clients at their best and worst. I am really excited that she has finally put these tips and practical "pearls of wisdom" into a book where we can all learn and appreciate the small and special tricks of new business that keep winners winning and keeps agencies growing. This book will be a best seller in the agency world – and I suspect that many aligned businesses will benefit from her thoughts and advice."

**- Johanna McDowell, Founder & CEO, Independent Agency Search and Selection Company**

"Most of us agency people who have been around for a lot of years are pretty good at new business...Lisa's Tweets will make you better!"

**- Brent Kuhn, Vice Chairman, BKV**

"This collection is both inspirational and practical, and perhaps most valuable of all, brief. "It is with words as with sunbeams, the more they are condensed, the deeper they burn." - Robert Southey.

**- Judith Carr-Rodriguez, Founding Partner & President, Figliulo + Partners**

"Following Lisa's tweets provides a true master-class education in cultivating relationships. Her book brings all those tips together and truly shows you how to win, in a way that you really just can't find anywhere else. I'm all about #newbusiness"

**- Andrew Graff, CEO, Allen & Gerritsen**

"Lisa Tweets like she plays piano: "allegro gracioso." Each of her daily #newbusiness Tweets gives us simple tips that should be obvious but are often forgotten. One of my favorites: "*We have two ears and one mouth to remind us to listen twice as much as speaking.*" Her book should be on the night table of every agency CEO or NewBiz officer for a night (re)cap before the pitch."

**- Herve de Clerk, Founder, AdForum**

"Tweets of business advice, I love it! For those of us working in an environment of mass chaos on a daily basis, abbreviated flashes of great thinking is a brilliant way to provide us bikini versioned ideas while staying relevant."

**- Carrie Zimmerman, Co-Founder and CEO, The Zimmerman Agency**

"In her excellent career guiding and steering important partnerships between agencies and clients Lisa has seen it all – from the truly remarkable, Great Winners, sublime and powerful

– to those who really should go and do something else altogether
... Her delightful way of sharing her first hand experiences of
the eternal quest to win great business opportunities is a treasure
trove of insight and wonderful stories that would help anyone
to sit back and think again. It is never too late to throw one's
knowledge away in the quest to learn something new and this
book will do just that. Read it over a long, slow brew."

**- Alexei Orlov, Global CEO , RAPP**

L2 Publishing
New York, NY

In order to adhere to the 140 character Twitter restriction, some Tweets may not be grammatically correct or have proper punctuation.

❤ Indicates a Retweet or Liked Tweet by followers.

 @AARLisa

#newbusiness

Colantuono, Lisa
@AARLisa: New Biz in 140 Characters (or Less).
Nuggets of Knowledge for Prospecting and Pitching smAARter

ISBN-13: 978-0692662274

This book is dedicated to my mother, Anna Colantuono –
you have taught me the power of prayer and perseverance
even in the face of extraordinary measures; to my father, Vito
Colantuono – you have taught me how to work harder than my
competitor; and to my nephew, Jake, and my niece, Juliana –
you have taught me the true meaning of unconditional love…
I love you both "to infinity and beyond!"

"Strange is our situation here upon earth. Each of us comes for a short visit, not knowing why, yet sometimes seeming to a divine purpose. From the standpoint of daily life, however, there is one thing we do know: That we are here for the sake of others...for the countless unknown souls with whose fate we are connected by a bond of sympathy. Many times a day, I realize how much my outer and inner life is built upon the labors of people, both living and dead, and how earnestly I must exert myself in order to give in return as much as I have received and am still receiving."
~Albert Einstein

# CONTENTS

| | |
|---|---|
| **FOREWORD** | **1** |
| **PREFACE** | **3** |
| **INTRODUCTION** | **5** |
| **PART I: INSIDE MARKETERS' MINDS** | **9** |

C-Suite Struggles
Top Priorities for Marketers
The "New" Consumer
Rationale for Reviews
Agency Essentials Marketers Must Have

| | |
|---|---|
| **PART II: CREATING CONNECTIONS THAT COUNT** | **41** |

First, Do No Harm
Treat Your Prospects Like Clients
Prospecting that Penetrates
PR that Pulls
Courting Search Consultants

| | |
|---|---|
| **PART III: THE PITCH** | **71** |

Pitch Tips (for Agencies of All Sizes)
Write to be Read: Gripping RFIs; Breakthrough Case
    Studies; Penetrating Self-Promotion
Chemistry is More than Just Physical Attraction
Work Sessions that Work
Speak to be Heard: Presentation Pointers
Final Pitch Factors
Insights About Incumbents
Deliberation Discussion

## PART IV: POST PITCH PURSUITS     103

Compensation that Counts
Leave Behinds that Matter
Treat Your Clients Like Prospects
Maintaining Ties that Bind

## PART V: NURTURING AGENCY ASSETS     119

Creative Firepower
Websites that Wow
The Value of Intellectual Property
Leading by Example
Culture Counts
Taking Care of Business

## PART VI: ADVICE FROM THE LEGENDS     151

Quotes from Teachers from Whom We Can All Learn

## PART VII: AS SEEN IN THE PRESS     161

Published New Business Articles by Lisa Colantuono

## CLOSING THOUGHTS     231

## THANK YOU & ACKNOWLEDGEMENTS     235

# FOREWORD

I'm a big fan of Twitter. I'm also a big fan of cutting through the crap and filtering out noise. Which may seem at odds with my Twitter fandom. Because Twitter is full of noise and b.s. It's been cluttered by self-promoters, snake-oil salesmen, charlatans and gurus, people who use lots of words – even on Twitter – and say very little. Some of these folks even churn out books of their Tweets. I'm sure you've seen some of them. I'm also sure you've never read any of them.

But you should read this one.

And I'm not just saying that because I'm a big fan of Lisa Colantuono. You should read it for the reasons why I'm a big fan of Lisa. In a vast ocean of obfuscation, she dispenses with the jargon and ten-dollar words designed to make our business seem more complicated than it is. She gets right to the heart of the matter in language so plain it's sometimes shocking to people who've grown accustomed to corporatized PR speak.

Lisa's presented at Advertising Age conferences and it came as no surprise that the audience hung on every word. Listening to her speak, I repeatedly find myself thinking "Exactly!"

Now, do an experiment. Open this book to any page and read a Tweet. Exactly!

There's a lot in this book, but you don't have to take it all in one sitting. Read a page here and there. Learn something new. Or be reminded of something you've forgotten.

1

Some of what Lisa writes you might already know. Hell, some of it you should already know if you're any good at your job. But in an age in which we're overwhelmed – by technology, by the news cycle, by email, by those ads that follow you around on the web it's understandable that we get distracted, that we forget some very basic things about our business.

Lisa will help you remember.

\- Ken Wheaton
Editor, Advertising Age

## PREFACE: For the ambitious bunch who squeeze out more than 24 hours in a day.

Read the press. Dig for opportunities. Update consultants. Meet with consultants. Make cold calls. Make follow up calls. Build relationships with the press. Write for the press. Brand the agency. Re-brand the agency. Track executive changes. Send out case studies. Develop relevant case studies for each prospective client. Create new collateral materials. Create credentials presentations. Develop a social media plan. Update the website. Filter inbound calls and emails. Develop prospect lists. Clean contact lists. Present to prospects. Attend conferences. Follow up from networking events. Write annual new business plans. Update online agency profiles. Write POVs. Write a book. Write newsletters. Write whitepapers. Respond to incoming calls. Write RFIs. Assemble the right team. Develop the pitch. Manage the pitch process. Et cetera, et cetera, et cetera....

Sound familiar?

Yes, it's the day in the life of a new business executive. And it isn't for the faint of heart. The pressure of this round-the-clock work culture – in which emails are expected to be answered at 11PM and cell phone calls taken on a Saturday morning – is the norm.

Yet new business executives are forever on the hunt for that silver lining – insights, tips and tricks to help increase the new business win rate. What works? What doesn't? Why or why not?

According to Amazon, there are more than 6,000 "new business advertising business books" that you can read to help you become the next Don Peppers (for those of you who don't know Mr. Peppers, he was one of the most famous and infamous business-development experts in the country more than three decades ago). Oh wait…what new business executive has time to read another long-winded, 300-page book?

New business executives are a special group wanting concise counsel extracted from headlines, posts and Tweets. *@AARLisa: New Biz in 140 Characters (or Less)* is precisely that…quick counsel in Twitter format. Chock-full of insights stemming from more than 15 years of managing a myriad of agency reviews at AAR Partners, @AARLisa is written for the time-starved new business executive who wants to learn (or be reminded of) the dos and don'ts on everything from marketers' pet peeves to prospecting pointers to the pitch process, but doesn't have the time to read page after page.

This flip-through, read-from-cover-to-cover, quick reference guide offers golden nuggets of knowledge and short-verse anecdotes from more than 1,300 Tweets in seven years for the on-the-run, 24/7 go-getter who wants the know-how with no more time added to the "not enough hours in a day" day.

**- @dickinsonchuck**
I'm a follower and like your Tweets because they are actionable and specific. I enjoy your lessons and views.

# INTRODUCTION

♥ **There's no magic bullet with new biz. It takes patience, perseverance and wanting to make a real difference for a particular brand!**

New business is the lifeblood of all agencies and when you're armed with insights from wisdom that only the years can bring, your success rate starts to skyrocket and failures become success turned inside out. Writing RFIs isn't a license to talk about "me." Instead, it is an opportunity to be invited to the first step of the review process by exemplifying how the agency's relevant experience will help solve the prospective client's marketing issues. By keeping the broad marketing issues in mind and talking about the prospective client, you will end up "writing to be read!"

Chemistry meetings aren't an invitation to talk about "me," either. They are an invitation for your agency to host a meeting enabling you to talk about category trends, consumer insights and business issues, all carefully wrapped in the agency's relevant experience so it will resonate. But the best teams often get left behind when authentic chemistry is lacking.

♥ **Failure to build the relationship by not demonstrating how you truly want to help their business will result in a lost opportunity.**

"I'm sorry," said the chief creative officer who was part of the team from a mid-size agency that was invited to a chemistry meeting for a prospective client "but I just flew back from Johannesburg after being out of the country for a week and I'm not even sure what your restaurant is about right now." Yet, he proceeded to try to answer the client's questions.

It didn't matter what his thoughts were on any topic about anything! After that opening statement, the entire client team wanted to walk out the door without saying another word. The meeting was over and the agency lost the opportunity to be invited to the next phase of the agency search regardless of their solid understanding of franchise systems, casual dining or anything else that was relevant to the prospect's business.

I don't care what time in the wee hours of the morning he landed back in the States, the first thing he should have done after going through customs was to learn something – *anything* – about the prospective client who was visiting the agency.

♥ **The only thing we sell is relationships.**

I have witnessed agencies being born and broken on pitching new business every year. I have talked to new business teams who spend ungodly hours working on the perfect pitch and new business departments that spend millions each year on what they hope will be a positive return on investment. But what makes one agency more successful over another? Sure, it's about understanding what really keeps clients up at night. Yes, it's about prospecting more intelligently and learning more about the business than just its marketing needs. But it all really comes down to relationships. Relationships built on credibility and trust. Building relationships is essential to develop a robust and thriving new business practice. It's a very simple equation: credibility + trust + relationship building = new business.

♥ **Passion is powerful. Everything else is the price of entry.**

And the key to strong relationships? Passion and chemistry. Nothing beats that combination. And you can't fake it or define it. If an explanation is necessary then the agency simply doesn't have it.

♥ **How to lose a pitch? Harp on proprietary tools and process! Nothing is "unique" except for your TEAM!**

I don't attend a single agency meeting that doesn't end with the question, "Who's hot and why are they doing well?" It's an interesting question since the answers are typically non-transferable. Why? Because each agency is unique! How? Because of their *people* <u>not</u> their proprietary processes!

I have been on the receiving end of hundreds of new business presentations over the years and I have also given many more in both the classroom and the conference room. As part of the AAR Partners team, I have counseled client teams evaluating final presentations and witnessed the agony over the final selection. I have been part of chemistry meetings, briefings, strategic presentations and creative presentations. And there is one thought that stands out the most. Many are not memorable, fewer are inspiring, and more fumble over mistakes from lessons forgotten long, long ago. We need to be quickly reminded of the little gems that help us prospect and pitch smAARt. And that's why I've written this reference book of new business lessons in 140 characters (or less).

## PART I: INSIDE MARKETERS' MINDS

♥ **1/2 of what is known today wasn't known 10 years ago & it's doubling every 18 months. Assist the next generation CMO w/change.**

As a result of this ever-evolving world, the role of the CMO continues to change rapidly. Long gone are the days of the traditional communications plan. The increasingly empowered and skeptical consumers are continuously placing new demands on the marketplace and calling the shots like never before. Technical skills are vital to pleasing these more demanding customers and understanding who they are on a behavioral level is critical.

Marketers are suffering from "infobesity" when it comes to the overabundance of data and its absorption. Marketers are inquisitive, experimental and innovative by nature but may not always have the resources or skill set necessary and many are still operating in outdated ways.

In addition to the data explosion, top challenges that keep marketers up at night include social media trends, proliferation of channels, digital-powered consumers and of course, making the brand relevant to the consumer in a saturated space. Is it any wonder why marketers are losing sleep?

Top challenges such as getting a grip on content development, understanding the connected consumer and keeping ahead of (or at least up with) the pace of technology are always top-of-mind. These marketing needs are big opportunities for agencies prospecting and stewarding clients, but smart agencies also keep in mind some of marketers' frustrations with agencies: selling technology and not the solution, over-emphasizing data without understanding the insights and not offering business solutions across disciplines.

♥ **"I want the agency to feel the soul of my brand!" Quoted from a marketer searching for an agency. #newbusiness**

Something that all agencies should keep in mind and it is analogous to the Hippocratic Oath taken by a physician: "First, do no harm." Marketers expect their agencies to share in the brand's need, offer proactive ideas, worry about their business the way they do and first and foremost – listen. The best agencies understand their success will come from taking care of their clients and helping them to become successful. The question that should be asked continuously is, "How can we help them succeed?" rather than, "What can we do to win (or keep) the business?"

♥ **Consumers have a Ph.D. in advertising today. Be sure to help marketers share their brand's authentic purpose. #newbusiness**

Today, the most successful brands win by bonding with consumers over shared goals and philosophies. Those purpose-driven brands that become the center of attraction rather than just attention are the ones that marketers are most intrigued by and often want to find out the agency behind the movement.

♥ **Major reason for agency review? Agency became complacent with the brand business.**

Marketers call reviews for a myriad of reasons but essentially all of the reasons fall into two main buckets: uncontrollable and controllable.

Uncontrollable reviews are typically brought about due to corporate mergers, realignments and consolidations, poor business management and executive changes. In most of these situations, the review is simply inevitable. The agency is not at fault.

Controllable reviews are very different; they are subjective in nature. Generally, they occur as a result of, or a perception of, lack of stewardship. Common reasons include: creative differences, absence of innovative ideas, lack of integrated communications plans, disconnect between strategy and creative, agency team turnover, a perception that the agency is more concerned with pitching than nurturing current clients, and the big one – complacency. All are avoidable issues if the agency is consistently growing and evolving with the marketer.

Marketers need agency talent and resources just as much as agencies want the brand on their roster. But there are certain must-haves for the CMO moving at the speed of change – real-time marketing, shareable stories, relevancy, measurement and experimentation – and agencies can be a powerful resource for all of them.

❤ **What do clients primarily want? Great creative and to be pushed to the next level. #newbusiness**

The new CMO must have a full-time team member consistently learning brand new platforms. Help them learn new media! #newbusiness

♥ **Marketer's frustrations? Some of the best creative work is being done by our consumers instead of our agencies! #newbusiness**

The #1 reason why clients call a review? Recent AMI study says work didn't achieve results. #newbusiness #BOLOCON

Don't react to the speed of culture. Become part of culture. Brand rules for a brand new world. #newbusiness

We must shift from AIDA to Provoke, Share, Connect, Own. #newbusiness

What worries marketers? Will the working relationship with the agency be too time consuming...? #newbusiness

♥ **The "pitch team" is a constant concern for mktrs in a review. Offer a guarantee that the team pitching is the day-to-day team! #newbusiness**

Today is about being able to A/B test creative and keep iterating. Help mktrs w/tech which is intimately connected to brands. #newbusiness

What concerns mktrs? Giving feedback & agency team feels as if they've been deflated. Be collaborative in all conversations! #newbusiness

4 vital needs w/a tech partner: Does the tech have legs? Add value over time? Consumer benefit? Price-value ratio makes sense? #newbusiness

♥ **What marketers want? Agency honesty. Don't just tell them what they want to hear. Push them. Make 'em nervous. #newbusiness #AASmallAgency**

Marketer's Needs? Internal efficiencies, innovation, consistent and meaningful messaging, building purposeful brands. #newbusiness

Inside the marketer's mind: "The brand must evolve via consumer insights & look outside our segment/industry for inspiration." #newbusiness

Address needs and desires but also anticipate where change may (and should) occur. #newbusiness

What do marketers want their brand to offer their clients? An authentic human touch. #newbusiness

Burning question from the prospective client POV? "Why do you want to work with our team and on our brand?" #newbusiness

♥ **Numbers alone aren't always accurate so be sure to put rationale & experience behind all analytics. #newbusiness**

What do marketers look for when selecting a new agency? An agency that doesn't make the client make assumptions. #newbusiness

No one person can manufacture it, market it and fund it. Figure out where to fill in the gaps and become part of it! #newbusiness

There's hope in something new...exemplify the optimism and

how a small change can bring new beginnings and better results. #newbusiness

♥ **Need three keys to have the competitive advantage: mastery; insights behind the facts; remain fresh. #newbusiness**

Relevant experience is necessary but ambition is vital! #newbusiness

"Offline is not even a concept" is the reality just around the corner... #forbescmosummit #newbusiness

Mktg principles haven't changed but tactics have...don't get caught up in tactics & stay focused on why consumers should select your brand. #newbusiness

Products are boring. People are interesting and they are part of the business solution. #ANAMasters #newbusiness

Digital and programmatic are great but the power of a truth and core creative idea trumps all tactics. #ANAMasters #newbusiness

♥ **Data is not data...it's people! #ANAMasters #newbusiness**

Scarcity - the less you reveal the more consumers want to know/ engage. i.e.: The most interesting man campaign. #ANAMasters #newbusiness

Purpose driven brands create value with values! #ANAMasters #newbusiness

♥ **Instant communications has led to impatience. Allow prospective clients to think, reflect and sleep on it...give them breathing room! #newbusiness**

A travel and tourism client was searching for a new advertising agency and AAR Partners was hired to manage the agency search. After a three-month process that started with many reputable ad agencies, the client narrowed down the universe to four top-notch finalists. After two days of listening to final pitch presentations and then debating, discussing and deciding on which group to select as the winning agency, it was a dead heat between two of the four finalists. The team of ten clients needed to sleep on the decision and requested that the agencies give them 24-hours to think.

That evening I received a call on my cell phone from the chairman of one of the four finalists. He is a well-seasoned executive who runs a multi-million dollar advertising agency and needed advice from me about what to do next. The answer was simple. I told him to do nothing and gave him specific rationale behind my answer. The client team was not made up of Type-A personalities who welcome the overly aggressive new biz exec gunning for their account. Although he trusted my advice, his personality got the best of him and he decided to approach the client once more during their deliberations. It worked against him and his agency lost the potential of a new account.

Move from programmatic to agile and addressable for efficiencies and effectiveness! #ANAMasters #newbusiness

Achieve simplicity out of complexity...consumers judge in a simple way. #ANAMasters #newbusiness

The impact of what mktrs do has been minimized by chasing short-term objectives due to an over-abundance of data. #ANAMasters #newbusiness

Clarity and consistency of brand promise is what makes good brands great. #ANAMasters #newbusiness

Data must not inhibit intuition! #ANAMasters #newbusiness

❤ **Brands need to reach us where we emotionally live and need to be meaningful to consumers' lives. #ANAMasters #newbusiness**

Finding your real brand purpose will keep you on purpose! #ANAMasters #newbusiness

Advertising is about orchestration not just integration. #newbusiness

❤ **The future of data analytics? Understanding humanity and authentic emotional connections. #newbusiness"**

If you're not in the business of offering business solutions then you need to find a new business! #newbusiness

Ideas anchored in data driven insights is a must to create enduring brand stories where characters become part of culture! #newbusiness

Don't settle for marcom plans that are primarily tactical & limited. Think strategically w/a bigger purview. Push boundaries. #newbusiness

Don't make decisions based out of fear and disguised as practicality. #newbusiness

♥ **Top Marketer Challenges? Increase ROI, Improve Digital, Leverage Social Media. #newbusiness**

It's more than cause-marketing...today success is based on cause-engagement. #newbusiness

True insights live in the heart but must be culturally relevant.

Three quarters of marketers believe that digital firms need to bring a full complement of offerings and not just creative digital skills.

U.S. CEOs are looking to go beyond the good experience to an 'always-on' customer experience.

♥ **Millennials are moving the industry at the speed of change...engage don't advertise! #ForbesCMOSummit #newbusiness**

Top attributes an advertiser wants from an agency: 1. strategically grounded, integrated campaign that effectively meets goals. 2. Reactive

Exemplify category expertise by showing how you've solved business problems for the brand.

No metrics no marketing but don't forget the vital piece of instincts!

CMOs report they spend 8% of marketing budgets on marketing analytics, and expect to increase this level in the next 3 years. (CMO Survey)

Help mktrs understand 'what's next' by bringing their consumers content re: trends in media, tech, culture, biz, entertainment & society.

♥ **Brands should no longer be nouns. Help marketers to turn their brand into a verb.**

Find the sweet spot between big data and emotional data... It's the human experience that is the most vital metric.

88% of CEOs believe getting closer to the customer is the top business strategy over the next five years, according to a recent IBM study.

Put the "Full" in Full Service: drive innovation of your offerings from clients' needs...saturate brands in media that matter & convert.

♥ **At the end of a day, people notice if you made a difference in their lives. Help mktrs listen to the "little things" that make a big impact.**

Empowered consumers make better products. Help your clients listen to their consumers for real time insights.

Help CMOs be great: Connect w/customers, bring in employees, connect to partners, & create connected products w/a competitive advantage.

Clients' concern with a mid-sized agency? Less access to deep data!

♥ **Marketers like the personalized service that comes with a smaller/midsized agency!**

Tight budgets & lack of clear online strategy keeping CMOs up at night! Top issue: acquiring/retaining customers + integrated experience.

Help CMOs with gaining greater visibility: relieve the fuzziness between investment and impact!

Predictive analytics are a must but they must turn into actionable insights.

The smartphone is the remote control for life. Be relevant on consumers' most important screen that's only "a pocket away!"

♥ **Common reason to call a review? Disconnect between strategy and creative execution. #newbusiness**

Do you have a clean slate brand? Consumers are attracted to new & unproven brands...perceived as faster, cleaner, transparent & responsive!

Conquer complexity. There is a vital need for simplicity and a simplified brand experience.

What do marketers need from agencies? Real-time, relevant, uninterrupted consumer engagement!

Show how you can help the brand to "stand out" but remember that consumers want to "fit in" & brand affinity is being part of that group.

Think bravely! Act collaboratively! Flexibility creates innovative ideas...be nimble!

♥ **Agency of the future must include: chief engagement officer, chief integration officer, chief mobile/metrics officer, chief data officer!**

How well does the agency team view its client's business through their consumers' eyes!?

Help clients to stop "telling and selling" and instead, encourage them to "engage and praise."

♥ **Approx. 25% of the time, agencies lose a prospective client since clients are concerned that they do not have sufficient market insights.**

## What do CMOs want? Insights, Innovation, Integration, Predictive Modeling and Metrics!

I've listened to many marketers discuss their needs, goals and worries. They all discuss the overload of data. Instead they want core insights from the data and want to be able to tell an emotive story. A past client of a QSR brand once said during the deliberation of selecting the final agency, "Marketing is all about experiential communication plans leading to human engagement which is based on behavioral insights. The agency that can offer this is the agency of the future."

It doesn't take 3 chefs to make a batch of cookies! Make sure your agency integrates well w/other agencies to create the optimal marcom plan.

Marketers struggle with integrating social media into the overall strategy. Only 6.8% believe social media is "very integrated" (CMO Survey)

**♥ Help marketers use data to vet decisions and not make decisions. #newbusiness**

60.2% of marketers are looking for analysis options and other analytics options in their social media management tools. Source: SEOmoz

Presenting creative? Great ideas also need excellent execution. Show both!

What typically causes an agency review? Flat creative; change in leadership; business performance issues; relationship problems.

Help CMOs & CEOs understand the efficacy of the marketing investment & reduce the chances of procurement embarking on an ROI evaluation

♥ **CEOs focus on internal communications as a key challenge/ opportunity. Help them ensure people understand & live their brand/company vision.**

CMOs vital issues? Budget reprioritization, social media impact, ROI pressure and sales function encroachment.

CMOs must communicate their vision & value positioning in the company. Help them articulate that vision!

Retail mentality is addictive to (current and prospective) clients.

What keeps CMOs up at night? Complexity of the marketplace and technology are two vital factors and powerful external forces affecting mktg.

♥ **What do CMOs need? Value that empowers consumers; enduring connections; analytics with insights.**

Don't show the same old traditional thinking. You must integrate digital in order to exemplify "tradigital" ideas.

What sparks a review? Breakdown in communication, senior team churn, complacency sets in.

Marketers' top priorities? Need to talk to consumers more effectively; create loyalty; stay competitive; effectively use digital media.

♥ **Mktrs want innovative ideas but are concerned about the complexity of execution. Show the idea and HOW it can be executed. #newbusiness**

Make friends of non-consumers. Offer something for nothing and they will come back for more that you offer.

Top client business needs: social media, ROI, brand insights, "tradigital" media.

Reasons for a review? Lack of creative spark; strategic/creative disconnect; digital incompetence; need an integrated plan.

What stories is your data telling you? Understand the customer, prospect and lapsed customers with each medium!

Social media is a key engagement channel but CMOs struggle with capturing customer insight from the unstructured content produced.

CMOs expect more complexity over the next 5 years. Help decipher the explosion of data & be keen on consumer insights!

♥ **Mktrs Needs? Digital marketing needs to cease... instead marketers need to shift to mktg to a digital world! #newbusiness**

What do clients want according to Michael Roth? Digital insights, total integration and accountability!

Customer centricity is a top corporate agenda item. CMOs want to know what customers want—even before customers know what they want.

CEOs want ideas with a capital "I" from marketing. Not the tinkering-around-innovation, but the kind that impacts the bottom line.

♥ **Act as the Chief Marketing Technologist for your client and help to integrate search, social and content in order to optimize results.**

Marketing today is a delicate mix of art & science, but from the POV of the corner office, the ultimate focus must always be the business.

88% of mktrs use social media BUT 72% have only started recently & need to know how to convert social media efforts into tangible results!

What does the marketer want from his agency? 100% integrated communications plan from collateral to social media!

♥ **Rationale for review? Creative ideas are great but execution is difficult, expensive and delayed. #newbusiness**

Top frustration with agencies: "inability to proactively think and act strategically."

CMOs want 3 social media metrics: social pulse (engagement, activity); purchase funnel (awareness, consideration); & results (leads, sales)

What marketers want from agencies? Creative, engaging ideas not just advertising plans!

♥ **Despite increasing spending on social media, marketers have a hard time proving ROI for this channel. Help them w/ analytics. #newbusiness**

Instead of offering marketers the "data dump" be sure to offer data designed with category/consumer/brand trends and insights.

What marketers want from agencies? Be strategic, innovative, proactive and think operationally!

CMOs agree that analytics are absolutely table stakes today...not just a nice to have!

Top 2 CMO needs: 1. Demonstrate profitable growth. 2. Shift from controlling the message to galvanizing consumers.

Insights are critical drivers of innovation & growth but less than 1/3 of mktrs use metrics to evaluate the quality of these observations...

Metrics is a must but first focus on great ideas that resonate with consumers...then maximize reach!

♥ **Marketers are looking for best in class agencies collaborating and executing an integrated fashion.**

Reasons to believe are reasons to purchase. Exemplify performance and progress since it provides "emotional functionality."

Switching agencies? Consider ALL costs. Relationships are often saved by 2-way evaluations ensuring clear understanding of the relationship.

What do clients want? Analytic capabilities to deliver insight, not just data, to help guide investment decisions.

❤ **You can't manage what you can't measure! Be sure to offer insights on analytics. #newbusiness**

Clients are looking for Relevance and Resonance regarding creative.

What do clients want from their agency? Exemplify how their consumer will see value in their brand in a unique way.

Even if consumers can be targeted en masse, there is a vital issue: engagement. Before you can connect with a consumer, help them notice you.

WWW isn't World Wide Web. It's Wherever Whenever Whatever. Don't build destinations. Reach consumers wherever they are…

❤ **Don't be the loudest brand in the sector…be the fittest brand instead. #ANAMasters #newbusiness**

3 vital mktg priorities: effectively maximize the mktg budget; support mktg innovation; need to be agile.

CMOs need to push for innovation experimentation but only with a serious focus on ROI!

♥ **The next wave of CMOs must reorient the company culture around customers. Help ensure consumer experience is consistent w/brand promise.**

Build a purpose-driven brand. Have your product mean more than a mere transaction for the consumer... Build stronger loyalty in the process.

**A sense of arrogance and entitlement...two reasons why the ad agency lost the client.**

Over the years, I've spoken with many clients about the potential of doing an agency review and there are many reasons for calling a search. In my opinion, this one takes the cake. When agencies start to think they know more about the brand then the brand managers or CMOs, clients aren't too pleased. "It is evident when neither account nor creative teams really listen to my needs. A sense of arrogance sets in where the agency believes they know more about the client's marketing goals than the client."
  - Gord Kerr, (past) Director Corporate Social Media,
    RBC Financial Group

It's the intersection of category, consumer and brand insights that ignites the Big Idea!

Engaging an audience online is a priority today. Keep commitment to digital less about display and more about participation.

Want to build a successful brand? Remember to add values to value!

Shed the habits we all fall into: complacency, conformity, analysis paralysis, hands-off management and knowledge silos.

♥ **Help mktrs sort through compelling stories about their brand & most importantly, help identify the right moment to share them. #newbusiness**

Adaptive mrktrs embrace new media and empower their teams to be involved in shaping the brand experience.

Extend brand reach through emotional interactions...create gentle collisions that don't leave the consumer like they've just been sold!

Buying impressions is irrelevant in today's user-centric world! Acquire user data instead and speak with (not AT or even TO anymore) the user.

♥ **True agency partners know more than one side the client's business. Focus on mktg but offer insights on operations too. #newbusiness**

Brand love and brand value must be intertwined. Think Zappos: targeted yet personal; JetBlue: focused yet engaging.

Consumers expect value and values from brands today! Be sure to offer both.

"Maturalism" is the new materialism - spending conservatively is more than just a trend.

♥ **Maximize the brand, not the channel. #newbusiness**

Corporations are developing programs that have an emotional attachment corporate social responsibility is part of their new fabric.

Mktrs must meet today's challenges with precision guided by insightful consumer analytics - who, what, where must be answered!

3 top issues for marketers: improving customer retention and loyalty, acquiring new customers and increasing sales to current customers.

Mktg today? Behavior first. Attitude second. Mktg that only depends on attitude changes is over...change a behavior NOT an attitude!

Listen to your customers. They like to offer advice if it means better brand experience...meaning stronger brand loyalty in the end!

Need to improve accountability? Align marketing activities costs with business goals.

♥ **25%+ of all Google searches now originate from smartphones...help brands leverage the power of mobile marketing.**

Are you giving off a sense of "entitlement" to your clients? Stop. Start listening. Show that you're an extension not that you're entitled!

Is your brand considered "participatory?" If not, it's time to start participating in this powerful form of communications!

Status Stories v. Status Symbols? Need to shift from brands telling stories to brands helping consumers tell their own status-yielding story.

♥ **Brands don't sell brands. People sell brands and they need a Reason to Believe! #newbusiness**

Clients want digital to be integrated with traditional media and not the whole solution. It's not just about the next new digital thing!

Branding in the Age of Social. Align your company your constituents' expectations/values not just in communications.

Top Concerns for Marketers: ROI, retention, loyalty!

If you engage your consumer and allow them to participate...they will own your brand!

Find the consumer insight and simplify the key message! That's what marketers want!

Is your brand a "butler?" Be sure your brand offers value to consumers by helping to lighten the load of their chaotic life-styles.

Empowered consumers, treated well, will become 10x more virally valuable than before...adapt new programs that sell to today's customers!

Often overlooked mktg gem: Relevance, specific to your target audiences, will help your advertising sell more of your products/services.

♥ **Factors influencing CMOs' decisions regarding which agencies to invite into a review? Previous relationships; peer referrals; agency reputation.**

TV 2019? No longer a shotgun approach. Persona-based TV will move advertisers closer to 1 to 1 mktg deep-dive targeting.

The digital world is changing how we deliver experiences & we innovate. It's also changing customers. Be sure to entertain & educate!

Is your brand handling experiential moments with its customers well? Brands must stand behind their promise reinforce brand value!

Judging creative work? Evaluate more with your heart than your head. Does the brand bond with you as a consumer and move you emotionally?

♥ **Help the CMO clearly understand how the brand experience is being delivered to consumers. #newbusiness**

In today's market, it's not about being cheap, it's about being relevant. Allow shoppers to know your brand is worth the price of purchase.

Need a new ad agency? Look for the agency who understands how your brand bonds with your consumer & marries traditional with digital!

The most important criterion to evaluate an idea: "Will it achieve its objectives?" Only 55% clients think their agencies share same viewpt.

54% of consumers feel that the barrage of irrelevant messages, low value rewards, impersonal engagements = brand defection!

Successful Brands = Create Preference (Intel) + Emotional Bonds (Disney) + USP (Gap)

How will your brand fall with the new value shopper? Focus on the behaviors that the shopper can control to reap the upside potential.

Can trading down seem like trading up? Can a higher price brand be a greater value? Make the consumer feel smart, not cheap.

❤ **Make the transactional more experiential. #newbusiness**

In the age of austerity, brands that will succeed are true to their core, reassure consumers, share positive values.

Are you just branding or are you bonding? Be sure to engage your audience build a relationship...at every touch point!

Branding? It's simply a set of promises made to your customer every time he interacts with you on your site, phone, e-mail, in-store, etc.

♥ **The day you stop challenging is the last day you're a challenger. #ANAMasters #newbusiness**

Don't get bogged down in price wars or imitating a rival's product. Redefine your market - invest a modest amount of energy into innovation.

According to Bain Co, 80% of CEOs think their brands offer superior experience. Only 8% of consumers agreed...talk to your consumers!

♥ **CMO success = automation + rich experiences. Help the marketer become a master of both. #newbusiness**

Link your products to your purpose. Believe in your product and customers will more readily deem it to be authentic.

Empower the people. Let your customers be your brand ambassadors and allow them to speak.

Support a cause that is connected to your business, meaningful to employees relevant to your customers to max the value of your reputation.

♥ **Moving from purpose to purchase can only happen with authentic brands that are not self-serving. #ANAMasters #newbusiness**

More than 50% of connected consumers make their 1st purchase from a brand due to a digital experience…opinions can be swayed online!

Don't try to "capture" an audience. Instead practice earned reach and consumers will reach out to you first.

Have a hot brand? Keep it at a steady simmer & it will become iconic instead of a fad. Don't flood the mkt…you'll lose your appeal.

CMOs recognize that social mktg affects nearly all forms of digital mktg; it shouldn't be treated as a silo. Think Skittles, Best Buy, Dell.

Loyalty program? Engage with brand's core customers learn how it can best serve their needs in a unique way from your competition.

Social Media Tip: Be interesting, experiment, make people want to talk about the topic. Keep it simple memorable.

Cultivate genuine open dialogue with customers. Listen learn. Respond with new features product innovations that match consumer needs!

❤ **Become a "questioner brand" in order to avoid being a challenger brand. #ANAMasters #newbusiness**

Integrate marketing efforts, motivate customers to interact with you AND share their personal networks with you…that's a powerful channel!

Measurement is vital for mobile social media but not at the expense of consumer experience.

Every phase of interaction determines how brands fare. Metrics used to perform analytics on, narrow in, act on info are in better position.

**Call reviews about the vitality of the relationship. Do not allow complacency to set in. Stewardship is vital...do not set & forget!**

When potential clients call the office to inquire about AAR Partners' agency search service, the first question I will ask is, "Why do you need to do an agency review?" After a few minutes of conversation, one particular hospitality marketer explained that she thought the incumbent's strategy was strong. She liked the creative. The media was solid. So I responded, "May I ask why then do you need to call a review?" Her answer was simple: "They don't worry about my business the way I do. They've become complacent and I feel like I'm the only one concerned about daily business troubles!"

Engage your audience. It's vital! Online banking customers were prepared to switch to banks that personalized their interaction.

**♥ Marketers allocate 7.6% of budgets to social media. CMOs expect that number to reach 18.8% in the next 5 years. (Source: CMO Survey)**

A brand gets "trust points" just for listening to customers. Be sure to listen and take action based on consumer input!

Sales reps have expanded from product specialist to solution seller. Know your consumers' buying habits and needs!

Losing loyal consumers is costly! "Evangelists" spend up to 20 times more on a brand than an average consumer.

What's old is new again...Twitter accounts being advertised on billboards newspapers! There is a need for TOTAL integration after all!

Build loyalty by encouraging conversation, even when users are unhappy with you. Don't bury heads in sand...try to control the conversation.

A successful CEO links the outside world with the inside world. Read 'What Only the CEO Can Do' in HBR by A.G. Lafley.

♥ **The acceleration of technology will breed mktg technologists. In the meantime, help clients market brands in a digital world. #newbusiness**

CMO or CDO? Chief Monologue Officer needs to become the Chief Dialogue Officer!

When you focus on customer retention, customer acquisition will happen.

It's not just about advertising. Connect w/consumers find the best way to use new options to get the right message to the right people.

♥ **Leaders are concerned with 3Cs that cause disruption: complexity, content and consumer experience. #ANAMasters #newbusiness**

Understanding "true innovation" during a downturn is critical. The expectations have increased...it must create VALUE to be innovative.

The need for now is critical! Understanding and implementing the importance of now is extremely relevant in today's market for all clients.

Just read 35% of marketers question the quality of online visitors. They're failing at converting interested visitors to leads!

Advice to CMOs - stick to your gut instinct.

The job as a marketer is to create tension. Find the edge of the table but don't go over it!

Marketing metrics is simple...profitable sales. Period. Look ahead more often than looking back.

Consumers say keep messages relevant! Keep them memorable. And keep them unobtrusive!

♥ **Data is just data w/o insights! #newbusiness**

3 keys for effective marketing? Open ear, open mind and courage to act decisively. #newbusiness

Engage consumers by keeping messages innovative and valuable for them.

Everyone needs to do much more with less. Kmart says earn more by producing results! Mktg must be an exchange of value.

What do CMOs want most from their agencies? Industry, brand, consumer insights...and of course, accountability!

♥ **What do marketers think agencies need to do to be more effective? Be as efficient as possible! Spend marketers' money like it's your own...**

Diversification of mktg options is a key challenge in the client-agency relationship. Evolve constantly and don't become complacent!

Agencies that understand challenger brands as well as taking calculated risks to make nickels spend like dimes are valued partners!

Growth is essential. Cost control is critical. And clients expect agencies to share the burden of being cost efficient. Be 100% transparent!

♥ **Listening is a lost art! Listen 2x as much as you speak and understand your clients' deepest concerns (that sometimes can't be verbalized).**

Client concern: "How does the agency keep its outside sister agencies truly involved on my biz if their expertise is needed for the biz?"

Be involved in the marketer's entire business, not just the advertising. Be a partner in the process from planning to execution.

Hiring a new ad agency? Ask them to define the future of advertising and what type of team they will need to accomplish what they say.

❤ **"I don't understand the focus on big data when we can't even get the little data right." #ANAMasters #newbusiness**

CMO's "managerial discretion" impacts stock values. And consumers today have power to constrain CMO's discretions. Include them in decisions.

Customers are expected to be less focused on price moving forward and more focused on innovation and brands being helpful.

According to experts on consumer behavior, the "new normal" will be about acquiring experiences...not things! Read Experience the Message.

❤ **Turn your brand over to your consumer. Then listen closely and respond quickly and genuinely. #ANAMasters #newbusiness**

## PART II:
## CREATING CONNECTIONS THAT COUNT

♥ **Prospecting isn't about selling. It's about finding opportunities to help new found friends.**

There isn't an agency that doesn't inquire about "the best way to prospect." Cold-call? Email? Snail mail? Blogs? Twitter? Attend conferences? Referrals? PR? And the list goes on and on. The one thing for sure is that new business is the heartbeat of every agency and strong relationships are the foundation of new business. Think about it. Would you rather work with someone you know, trust and like or someone you're taking a chance on and hoping for the best?

♥ **Large companies like Coca-Cola implement answering systems to filter out cold calls! Prospecting is pointless w/o offering valuable info.**

The days of "dialing for dollars" are long gone. Caller ID put the final nail in the coffin on that game. AAR Partners managed a review for Qdoba and the first time I called the client I was working with on the agency search, he answered the phone with much hesitation. When I asked if something was wrong, he responded, "No. I'm sorry. I didn't recognize your number on the screen, and I almost didn't answer the phone since I don't have time for a sales pitch!"

Nonetheless, prospecting is a necessary evil and it boils down to creating connections that count. How? The four Ts: Teach,

Trust, Touch Base, Timing. Sure, warm leads are always the best way to go about uncovering new business quicker, but successful companies keep building relationships on a consistent basis and never stop *teaching*.

**Teach:** When you teach something you instantly become a resource. Demonstrate your knowledge of what's happening with their primary competitor or industry. Offer ideas, insights and information about highly relevant topics. Sound like a trusted friend who has been thinking about their business issues – and one who truly cares!

**Trust:** Teaching builds credibility and credibility builds trust – instantly. And most clients want to work with people they can trust not just on an ethical basis but with a day-to-day, in-the-foxhole, I've-got-your-back mentality.

**Touch Base:** Stop "checking in" with no real rationale. Touch base for a reason. Share new insights, re-emphasize any business value that's been pre-established, continue to educate – share relevant articles and add your POV.

**Timing:** It's the old cliché of being in the right place at the right time, but you need to offer the right resources too. And that's where consistency takes the stage. It's been said that new business is a marathon and not a sprint. It takes time to create connections that count and part of that means reaching out at the right time. But it's not all guesswork. There are a number of specific, rational, "timing triggers" that help increase your chances of success. For example, new executives in position often means a re-evaluation of agency relationships; or a current media review can eventually lead to a creative review; or vacant CMO positions allow the potential opportunity to become an "outside" extension of the marketing team to help fill the current void.

♥ **New biz is everyone's business but be sure to have a dedicated person committed to it or it quickly becomes no one's business. #newbusiness**

The ideas are endless and there is no secret formula for winning new business – just perseverance, passion and authentic concern about the prospect's business challenges that you can help to resolve in an innovative, integrated, insightful manner. Immerse yourself in their business. Join their associations, attend their conferences, get their newsletters and dig into their websites. Figure out how their category, consumer, brand, or marketing challenges are a match for your capabilities and expertise and leverage that. And no matter what, make sure you have one key person who is responsible for new business. It's only then that you can start creating connections that count!

How to get your agency to stand out from the crowd? Launch a comprehensive PR campaign and don't be afraid to self-promote. #newbusiness

♥ **Want to engage a prospect quickly? Tell a relevant story. Our brain is wired to co-create when a story is being told. #newbusiness**

Word of mouth is the single greatest influencer on purchase. #newbusiness #BOLOCON

Are you paying a search consultant to keep your agency credentials listed in a database or to consider you for a review? STOP! #newbusiness

Focus your attention on either sales or service...not both. #newbusiness

♥ **Prospecting? Talk about recent creative ideas that aren't ads at all and tie them to the prospect's brand needs. #newbusiness**

There's a difference between wanting an airline account and wanting "American Airlines" on your roster. Answer why THAT brand? #newbusiness

There's a difference between "wanting" a new client and "needing" a new client. Why do you WANT the business? Be honest. #newbusiness

♥ **Stop "checking in" w/prospects! There's nothing of value that's being added. Touch base to teach! Share something of interest. #newbusiness**

Address needs and desires but also anticipate where change may (and should) occur. #newbusiness

Network w/ "dormant ties" - people from your past. Time investment is low & the return greater based on pre-established trust. #newbusiness

**♥ Develop a relationship with a search consultant before the floodgates open and you hear of a review they're managing. #newbusiness**

Agencies are notorious for knocking on search consultants' doors for the first time when they hear or read about an agency review that has been launched. The problem is that it's typically too late. 90% of the time the review is already well underway or the universe list was already developed and approved. For example, I was recently involved in an airlines review. It wasn't more than five minutes from when the review was announced in the press to the time of the first phone call inquiring about the search. And for the next 48-hours, I received nothing but phone calls, emails, texts and Facebook messages from agencies asking to be considered for the review. Of course, the agencies that had the most difficulty were those who didn't have a pre-established relationship with AAR Partners. It's tough enough to build relationships and to help consultants keep your agency top of mind. When you try to prove your credentials at the time of the flood, it's close to impossible to be considered.

Two vital Qs to answer before pitching: What is the prospect looking for and, just as important, why are they doing a review? #newbusiness

♥ **Prospecting? Rule#1: Be Consistent. Learn how to generate leads with social media. #newbusiness**

It's not about seeing things as they are but rather as they could be...just provide true insights and courage. #newbusiness

Add a hashtag to your email campaign & allow prospects to move seamlessly to your social media conversations. #newbusiness

Having a creds meeting? Make sure you answer the question, "What can we do for YOU?" #newbusiness

People who share your passion & want to hear from like-minded people are your best prospects. Do your HW before reaching out. #newbusiness

♥ **Don't be the center of attention. Instead, be the center of attraction which will turn leads into action! #newbusiness**

Don't appear desperate. The prospective client needs your expertise just as much as you would like to earn their biz! #newbusiness

♥ **We have two ears and one mouth to remind us to listen twice as much as speaking. #newbusiness**

Strengthen current client relationships...offer a timely white paper and show that you proactively think about their business. #newbusiness

Shift the credentials presentations to capabilities conversations with prospects. #newbusiness

❤ **Great presentation skills don't trump great content. Focus on the conversation, passion for the brand & build a relationship! #newbusiness**

Prospecting? It needs...no, it MUST feel personal! #newbusiness

Remember that transactional selling only creates vendor relationships. #newbusiness

What does your agency look for in a prospect in order to have a successful client-agency relationship? Be specific! #newbusiness

If you want prospects to listen you need to remember HAIL: honesty, authenticity, integrity, love to help others. #newbusiness

Be a wingman. It says so much without saying a word. #ANAMasters #newbusiness

❤ **Replace the presentation with a conversation and prospect more successfully! #newbusiness**

Are you trying hard or competing hard? Don't try. Compete. When you compete you figure out innovative ways to stand out! #newbusiness

If the prospective client stands on your shoulders, can he see more clearly into the future of his brand? #newbusiness

**♥ Stay ahead of the curve but don't go flying around the bend with prospects! #newbusiness**

You won't convince anyone of anything w/a rational argument. Instead, convince w/emotional arguments & support it rationally. #newbusiness

There's a fine line between full service and ambulance chasing! Ambulance chasing is a slippery slope. #newbusiness

**♥ All choices bring consequences so be selective with the brands you choose to work with at your agency. #newbusiness**

Prospecting? Let your personality shine through when reaching out and you'll connect with them on a human level. #newbusiness

Want prospects to take action? Make them happy! Joy/happiness = drivers of action (i.e. the more positive an article, the more viral it is.)

Are you building true relationships with online communities? Be sure that you transform social monitoring into social caring!

**♥ While speaking with the VP of mktg at a QSR company, he mentioned he gets 100+ cold calls PER DAY. Think twice before you pick up the phone!**

The greatest fear should not be of failure, but of succeeding at things that don't really matter for a successful partnership!

"Who do you look up to, look forward and chase?" Matthew McConaughey didn't realize he also gave 3 great questions to ask when prospecting!

Don't just answer the prospect's question. Listen for the underlying meaning/request behind the question!

♥ **Instead of knocking on doors, build better relationships and slip in through the back door!**

Don't sell value. Show the value of what you can accomplish for your clients. Exemplify the outcome & not the perceived value!

♥ **What do seasoned new biz execs do differently? They prospect PROACTIVELY not reactively**

Big difference in being the center of attention vs the center of ATTRACTION. Attract prospects to you by being informative in real-time!

From the mouth of a marketer: "Establish a mutual interest before talking money!"

Don't tell and sell. Teach and share instead!

3-page pitch deck: Infographic snapshot of prospect's situation; initial category/consumer insights; overview of current consumer thoughts.

Roper Public Affairs: 80% of biz decision-makers prefer info via articles, not ads. Offer valuable content to attract your prospect.

Don't practice "random acts of sales support!" Disjointed efforts lead to sales inefficiencies. Timing is everything and proper tools help!

♥ **If you decide to decline a new biz opportunity, be transparent & consider offering suggestions to help the client's initial needs at hand.**

Brands are extensions of our personality & reminders of who we are (want 2b). Remind mktrs that they don't make stuff. They make MEANING!

♥ **There is only one thing that anyone can sell...relationships! #newbusiness**

Sell the outcome of the service you will provide...not the service alone.

3Es to new business: Educate (right info at right time); Engage (reminder of benefits and value of relationship); Enlighten (make it simple)!

Don't sell. Create fans by offering valuable information and let them become the medium for sharing your sales message.

♥ **Agency growth shouldn't always be a primary goal. Agency health first. Love who you're pitching; be selective. #newbusiness #AASmallAgency**

Don't compare. Every problem is unique. Learn from the past, focus on the now and solve the current problem to the best of your ability.

Humanize your work. Offer something only you can create. When you're a trusted source offering something unique you have value!

Return on Emotion results in Return on Investment. Show ideas that engage and influence...

Prospective clients don't just buy "what" you do. They also buy "why" only you can do it!

♥ **There is value in "I Don't Know" for current and prospective clients. #newbusiness**

The Future of Advertising is the same as present day. Tell unique & compelling stories that resonate & connect brands with their consumers!

Best way to get the attention of a prospect is through a personal referral...and make sure you have something vital to share!

♥ **Inspire others through witness in order to grow together by communicating. Fuel growth by attracting not proselytizing. #newbusiness**

Someone else can always do it for cheaper! Make sure you highlight the VALUE of why you can do it better!

Want to stand out when having initial conversations with a prospect? Talk diagnostics! Don't offer predictable solutions. Be inquisitive!

Be ahead of the curve for clients but keep the drive under control! Don't frighten them by speeding from A to Z too quickly...step by step.

♥ **Avoid the pitch! Follow people on the move, historical reviews, trends in categories, offer deep consumer insights... and do project work!**

Remind your clients to connect "directly to the neighborhood." Use store associates instead of actors whenever possible.

Be sure to put yourself in the marketer's shoes. Think about the complexities & variables on the client side & help offer biz solutions!

♥ **No one is more motivated to care about new biz than the agency owner! Stop hiring cold callers & build relationships yourself! #newbusiness**

Clients look for category experience but bring in fresh thinking from another sector and make it relevant.

Turn audiences into clients by making sure your work is tangible through examples. And don't forget to follow up after the presentation!

Linear relationships flatten fast! Don't just add to cognitive overload. Offer relevant information that resonates!

Mere interaction doesn't build relationships. Shared values build relationships!

❤ **The first principle of prospecting is understanding the pain point. And the first principle of offering aid is respect. #newbusiness**

I had a conversation with four CMOs at a conference one evening and I asked, "What are some of the ways that agencies prospect that irks you?" Each one of them talked about how agencies tend to send "generic or blanketed" collateral materials claiming how they understand their marketing pain points. "They don't know my pain points and saying they understand them when they don't just turns me off." One marketer had angst over a certain beetle eating the trees needed to produce the product his company sold. Another marketer's vital pain point was keeping the restrooms clean at the restaurants. Point being, agencies wouldn't know these specific and real marketing issues. Instead of making "generic" claims about their brand, talk to marketers about their consumer and what consumers want from their brand rather than sending all-purpose fluff.

Prospecting? Turn consumer insights into client business opportunities when reaching out.

❤ **Prospecting? Let great work attract clients and great content create buzz.**

Category experience or business smarts? Show both w/o being too tunnel-vision regarding the relevant sector experience.

Be sure to connect others to the desired end result before turning ideas into a concrete reality.

♥ **Great clients make mediocre agencies strong/weak clients make great agencies ineffective. Help mktrs be involved w/the agency. #newbusiness**

How do you keep prospects involved? Weave joy and surprise throughout the conversation to keep them engaged.

What are the 2 top characteristics that prospects look for when you're pitching them? Integrity and Passion.

What is the single most important thing that prospects are evaluating when you're pitching them? YOU!

♥ **"Yes...and" builds momentum and working relationships. Exchange "no...but" for "yes...and" in your prospecting. #newbusiness**

Addressing a conflict? Think about the 3rd side of the conflict which reminds both sides what's really at stake.

There's a huge difference between forging relationships and bombarding marketers for business! Follow up but don't become a stalker.

♥ **Just answer every question with depth and authenticity for a prospect. Don't try to close the sale on every call! #newbusiness**

~25% of reviews are managed by search consultants. Get to know the primary group but constantly forge relationships directly with marketers

♥ **The secret to getting a big win? Get a handful of small wins first. Little achievements build momentum, motivation & press! #newbusiness**

Following up? Consistent but gentle follow ups are fine. Don't be overbearing. It comes off as desperate...

Trying to get marketers' attention? Foster relationships - don't sell! Offer relevant thinking that resonates.

Don't solve prospect's problems too soon! Be a sounding board, offer general industry insights. Be objective, sincere and trustworthy!

Don't denigrate the competition. Sincerely compliment your competitor(s). When you do you set your own firm at a higher level.

Prospecting? Look for and use news about your prospects. Press mention is a good excuse for a personal note.

♥ **Prospecting? You must open the door & talk business. Only agency owners can truly do both! Stop hiring external cold callers. #newbusiness**

According to MarketingSherpa: 80% of decision makers reported that they FOUND their vendors. Concentrate on INBOUND not outbound marketing!

Prospecting Approach: Who are you talking to? Who is the competition? How do you want the prospect to feel? What do you want them to learn?

Want to get noticed? EARN the position of a "thought leader" and TEACH something with a USP!

❤ **75%+ marketing decision makers find their vendors, not the other way around. Become the center of attraction not attention! #newbusiness**

Prospecting? Become a specialist not a generalist.

Need to get to the next level in new biz? Stay in tune with start-ups & trends, attend panels outside the industry & LISTEN!

Sending info to a prospect? Be crystal clear, concise and value-oriented.

❤ **Think about brand purpose but think even more about your legacy...how you spend your time and with whom. #ANAMasters #newbusiness**

Sending an email to a prospect? Be clear, concise, include contact info and avoid empty flattery!

Prospective clients remember close to nothing about your credentials & almost everything about your thoughts on their category & consumer.

❤ **Whatever the problem, be part of the solution. Ask questions but make more statements (instead of pointing out obstacles). #newbusiness**

Prospecting? Speak to their customers, distributers, clients and gain some deep insights before making that first call!

Prospecting? Be a thought leader. Hold a free seminar on a mktg tactic that key prospects might be interested in finding out more.

Prospecting? Identify industry sectors where your team is already well versed and could build on that expertise.

Shark or service-provider? Sharks are shrewd & attack. SPs put others first. Their personal agenda is solving their prospect's problems!

♥ **Don't just accommodate your prospect's wants. Anticipate their needs and address them before they realize they want it.**

Win war w/o going to battle! Consistently set up "under the radar" visits w/prospects to build relationships, trust & kwldge about each other!

♥ **Identify the prospect's personal passion and offer them knowledge on how to pursue and fulfill it! #newbusiness**

Want more new biz? Calls, events, mailers, and metrics are all part of a vital SIT (stay in touch) system.

Silence speaks volumes! Don't drone on & on about your creds... present relevant experience, build trust and resonate with prospect's issue!

♥ **Three keys to a successful elevator pitch: passion, proof of traction and explanation of personal expertise.**

Profile your prospect to know who should be the lead account rep! We like people who meet our objectives & are compatible in personality!

Profile your prospects and determine if you need to focus on process, results, relationship or inspiration!

Following up? Don't be overly-aggressive. Don't knock on the door with little value. Don't pester the prospect. It's all too desperate!

Interact, inform, intercept...just don't interrupt!

CMOs need the CliffNotes version of what makes the agency unique...wow them in 20 minutes or less!

Simple Sales Approach: rehearse opening, ask 4 high-value ?s, offer concise relevant solutions, ask for follow up in-depth conversation.

The one question that can kill your sales conversation cold: "What is your budget?"

**♥ Prospecting? Make your efforts more people-focused and less conversion-focused. #newbusiness**

True there's more new biz movement but the economy is still turbulent! Grow your clients' revenues. Be proactive, inventive & spend wisely!

♥ **Want to prospect smAARter? Become a trusted source by building relationships w/faceTIME so you become the 1st call for help. #newbusiness**

Anchor strategy in creative; integrate creative across platforms BUT most important be an authority in the client's industry first!

Make the first face-to-face meeting interactive by creating an experience with the prospective client.

♥ **Connect and Converse in order to Convert...it's not about Convincing anymore!**

Anticipate. Don't react. It's the secret to Apple's success!

Drop the agency creds pres! The agency does 90% of the talking; the client does 10% which equals death 100% of the time.

Be quick to listen and slow to speak with current and prospective clients!

Interruption with innovation can gain interest. Disruption will not.

50% still generate new business the old fashioned way: refer a friend and "shaking new hands."

♥ **Prospecting? Send articles that are of interest and informative with your POV. Share...don't sell! #newbusiness**

Reminder...new business prospecting is a building block approach that takes time to manifest. It's not instant gratification!

Social media is just that...social. Socialize don't sell and the sales will happen.

Be sure to exemplify WHY the client needs to step out of its comfort zone for brand growth!

**♥ Posting content as part of your prospecting strategy? Don't post anything unless you deem it worthy of paying to distribute. #newbusiness**

Customer service is more than mgng complaints companies avoiding them. Listen, learn help... Google United Breaks Guitars ASAP!

Showing creative to a prospect? Show insightful, innovative and integrated work with ROI!

**♥ Prospecting? Mktrs want you, your insights, your team (not proprietary process) & how you make them feel about their brand. #newbusiness**

"Typically, the ratio of unscreened suspect-to-prospect=10:1, with a prospect-to-sales ratio=3:1. Meaning the suspect-to-sales ratio=30:1."

**♥ Never forget human touch: limit automation for outreach. Follow up w/ handwritten notes, personal calls, visits. They do stand out.**

Create value propositions by showing the difference between preference and parity...exemplify proof points!

**Serving lunch? Integrate it into the mtg by making it meaningful instead of just serving the expected sandwiches.**

Breaking bread has always been a great way to build bonds and although agencies clamor for a lunch meeting, they typically fail to make the most out of it. Sure, a nice spread across one side of the conference room is appreciated but something falls short about grabbing a sandwich and forcing conversation at the conference room table. During a review for a QSR client, one of the semi-finalists decided to split the group up into four teams. Each client team went to one of their competitor's locations with an agency team member to buy lunch, scope out the eatery and have some idle chit chat during the walk to and from the lunch location. When all teams returned to the agency with their lunch in hand, everyone ate together but also discussed the pros and cons of the client's competitors that they just visited to buy their lunch.

Prospecting? 1. Don't prospect everyone. 2. Are they good for you? 3. More importantly, are you good for them?

**♥ Exemplify how you're innovative and invigorating by sharing ideals (not just ideas) with prospective and current clients.**

Sell dreams not your services.

More Referrals? Ask! Ask a current client for a referral while working on their project...that's when the relationship is at its strongest!

Value Proposition that Sells: Resonate, Differentiate, Substantiate.

❤ **Prospecting? Potential clients want you to be an explorer not just an expert. #newbusiness**

Never send a non-personalized mailing to a prospect. It's your 1st chance to start bldg a relationship. It can't be done with "junk mail."

Prospecting? What's your agency's core strength? Can it be expanded? And is it transferable into other categories?

Prospecting? Be patient but gently persistent. New business is relational and takes time to come to fruition.

❤ **Do you understand your client's internal pressures? And more importantly, does your client know you understand their pressures? #newbusiness**

Build your business on live concerts, not album sales...in other words, do speaking engagements rather than just sending out credentials!

Has your brand hit an unexpected event? Don't sit quiet. If a negative online conversation occurred it must be addressed ASAP!

❤ **Referrals are the top new business generator. Are you doing what it takes to generate quality referrals? #newbusiness**

Don't sell. Educate!

Not closing enough new business? Provide client solutions, experience and relationships that work! Period. End!

"Ditch the Pitch" 86 the about-us monologue! Tell your agency's brand story by detailing cases proving expertise, insights, sales impact.

Small ad agency trying to crack the clutter? Project work is great for developing relationships allowing prospects to experience thinking!

Needs-based selling must be shifted to value-based selling. Offer engaging, sector-savvy viewpoints and diagnostics for your prospects.

❤ **Build stronger relationships by picking up the phone instead of hitting send. #newbusiness**

Prospecting? Upgrade analytic skills; become an insight enthusiast. Exemplify how your knowledge is relevant to your prospects' problems!

Is "everyone" in charge of cultivating new business? If so, then no one is responsible. Dedicate ONE person to stewarding new biz activities

❤ **When prospecting a new piece of business, ask yourself: Can I make a difference and why? #newbusiness**

Remember to lead people...not results. Be open honest; encourage motivate; lead by example!

Prospecting? Most global profits come from turbulent industries. Consider these profit pools: media, telecom, autos, airlines, financial.

3 obstacles for email campaigns: lack of available names; being labeled a spammer; notion that prospects don't want to be contacted that way

♥ **The biz problem may be obvious but you need to dig deeper to find out what's holding back the solution. #newbusiness**

Selling something? Be a Business Advisor: find the best answer for the problem, even if your service isn't part of the solution.

Want to get better results from your email campaigns? Tell a compelling story to effectively convey a call to action.

Networking = building+sustaining meaningful beneficial relationships w/people by focusing on how you can help THEM succeed/prosper.

"Nothing Personal…It's Just Business." Successful sales pros believe otherwise. People buy from people they like & trust… that's personal!

Know what you're looking for in a prospect. It's key to finding more opportunities, more revenue better ROI…know your ideal prospect.

♥ **Everything you do should be a reflection of the true you when prospecting and pitching! #newbusiness**

Prospecting for new business? Dialing for dollars is dead! Differentiate your offering, articulate expertise, don't target the masses!

♥ **Prospecting? Start thinking "team of record" instead of AOR! #newbusiness**

Prospecting? Create ongoing relevant dialogs with your prospect by offering valuable information...welcome to the engagement economy!

Leaving voicemails for prospects? Develop a series of VMs that leaves a different piece of information about your service.

Prospecting? Be selective! Don't pitch anything and everything. Match cultures. Be INTERESTED! And remember...it's NOT a one-way street.

Don't persuade...influence. Don't push...pull. It's not a monologue or dialogue...it's a "trialogue" but be sure to lead the conversation.

♥ **Stop selling credentials and start offering solutions (re: category, consumer, brand)!**

When leading buyers toward a sale, don't overdo the product analysis. Let consumers trust their instinct which may help reduce buyer remorse.

New Biz is like all other forms of sales. #1 Know your product inside out. #2 Understand relationship. #3 Be genuine.

2 main sources of new business. #1: personal referral/recommendation. #2: timely approach (Right prospect, right time, right message!).

♥ **Prospecting? Don't show how your agency can solve every problem because it can't! Show how you're solution-oriented with relevant examples.**

Would you call a prospect every day to pitch them? Don't send pitch emails every day either. Frequency is vital but don't stalk the prospect.

♥ **Stop "selling!" #newbusiness**

Sending a mailing to a prospect? Keep it short, to the point and demonstrate VALUE.

Prospecting? Show the prospect new ideas backed by research and validate how you intend to produce results.

Get rid of one-size-fits-all emails! Now is the time to tailor. Find tailored ways to move each prospect toward a sale by offering value!

♥ **There's no magic bullet w/new biz. It takes patience, perseverance & wanting to make a real difference for a particular brand! #newbusiness**

Better prospecting method? Let prospects find you instead of you finding them. Tactfully be in front of those interested in your expertise.

Stop talking start listening. The objective: listen your prospect into buying.

♥ **Want to stand out from the crowd? Truly love what you do. There's no faking it!**

Being a David is an advantage over being a Goliath in this economy. Be smart about your strengths wise about your weaknesses. Be honest!

♥ **Prospecting? Talk about recent creative ideas that aren't ads at all and tie them to the prospect's brand needs. #newbusiness**

36% of perceived value of a product is based on the sales person. Be truly interested have your prospect's best interest at heart..always!

"Do business with smart people. In fact, don't do business with "sales people." Instead, do business with business people. Buy a vision!

Prospecting cannot be rushed! Period. End. They make their own decision on their OWN time. Just be in their line of sight...

Prospecting Blues? Be consistent, value-oriented, and patient!

♥ **Help search consultants remember who you are and what you do...share newsworthy and brief emails about the agency quarterly. #newbusiness**

In business, we often need answers yesterday. But don't clamor for instant results during a sales process. Allow for time!

**Always be armed with knowledge. Knowledge builds credibility. Credibility builds trust. Trust builds successful relationships.**

I'm consistently asked by agencies about the best prospecting method. Frankly, there is no one best way to prospect. Similar to the way agencies talk about an integrated communications plan for clients, it's the same for their own brand…their agency. Treat your agency the way you would any brand. Develop an integrated marcom plan and apply reach and frequency to your plan. Here are two vital keys: make sure it's personalized to the individual you're sending to and be sure to teach something of value. When you teach (whether it's writing for the press, public speaking, sharing POVs, etc.) you're building credibility by sharing knowledge. And when you build credibility you build trust. That trust is what builds successful relationships and in turn, wins new business. So what works? All of it including writing for the press, speaking opportunities, email campaigns, follow-up calls, blogs, commenting on posted articles with your insights, attending conferences, mailings and more – of course, all within an integrated and strategic communications plan. As many clients have said to me over the years…when agencies reach out at the right time with the right message, I'm open to hearing what they have to say about how they can help my brand.

Find out the personality type of who you're prospecting: the quick decision maker, the #'s guy or the relationship guy who needs a partner.

❤ **Don't try to just get noticed…get talked about instead. #newbusiness**

Prospecting for a "whale of a client?" Don't. Find a client that you can turn their brand into a whale. It's a much more impressive story!

It's pretty clear. Marketers HATE the oversized direct mail pieces with no real supportive content!

Prospecting? Let your personality shine through when reaching out and you'll connect with them on a human level. #newbusiness

Don't think you need a signature in your email? Think again. Turn it into a marketing tool. Make it easy for prospects to get in contact!

❤ **Networking is an ordinary part of new biz efforts but helping industry folks in transition is extraordinary & rewarding in more ways than 1.**

Want more ink in the press? Be intentional w/an ongoing effort to get the agency name in the marketplace...make PR a priority!

Forrester trends presentation: third trend is customer advocacy will be the strongest driver of loyalty. Great example is Charles Schwab.

Want to get on the radar? Get in the press! Write informative articles that are not self-serving.

Want PR? Start with bloggers. People read trust blogs. Bloggers have influence on traditional media can lend credibility to businesses.

## PART III: THE PITCH

♥ **The pitch is a culmination of all meetings throughout the review process. It's the final pitch that should leave the prospect wanting more.**

Three months of research, strategy meetings, creative development, briefing, work sessions, cold pizza, late nights, weekend work and it comes down to a two-hour final pitch meeting to win the account. Right? Wrong. The pitch started 12 weeks prior when you first submitted the agency's RFI. The client evaluated your written responses: Do they have relevant experience? How engaging is the creative output? Is the culture similar to the client's internal culture? What about the level of enthusiasm oozing from the written submission? Out of a universe list of at least 15-20 agencies, they choose a handful to move forward as semi-finalists to meet with at chemistry meetings.

♥ **What's important in a chemistry meeting? Team interaction, relevant experience, general insights into the client's business & chemistry!**

Ah, the infamous chemistry meeting. Isn't chemistry supposed to feel natural and relaxed? So how is it that a formal chemistry meeting helps clients judge an agency's "chemistry" all within a 90-minute window? It always felt a little contrived to me but nonetheless, agencies are being judged on the internal group's chemistry and external chemistry with the prospective client by the prospective client. Why is this particular team at the

71

table, and what can this team offer that no one else can? Do they complement or contradict each other? Do they think as a cohesive unit? Are there any divas at the table? Are they listening?

The agencies selected to move on from chemistry will now be judged and scrutinized on everything from the questions they ask, to the insights they discover and thinking they provide, to the welcome mat at the front door, to the insightful thinking throughout the remainder of the process. And if the agency team doesn't keep up the chemistry and enthusiasm, the points start getting deducted fast. Let me be clear, pitch-theater just for the sake of pitch-theater – which can be lots of fun to see – doesn't go too far but pitches are won and lost on chemistry. Whether it's during a Q&A conference call, work session or work-in-progress check point, chemistry is continuously evolving and being evaluated along with how the agency addresses the needs of the client.

Yes, the pinnacle of the process is the final pitch. The entire client team is in attendance (even if they didn't participate throughout the entire review process) and the onus is on the agency to ensure that all client attendees are up-to-speed and on the same page. Not an easy task. You need to recap how far you've come, how much you've learned, how well you've listened, what you've uncovered and present a few options with one real recommendation with very specific rationale that you stand behind 150% and have the conviction that there is no better alternative. And then you…WAIT.

♥ **Final question a client asks before selecting the winning agency? "Can I entrust them with my brand?" #newbusiness**

Most agencies would love to be a fly on the wall in the deliberation room. What happens behind those closed doors? I've been part of these final discussion and selection meetings since 2001, and they can get heated. I will let you in on a little secret – it typically comes down to two agencies that the client team can't decide between. In fact, there was one review where there was a deadlock on the final two and the decision came down to a pros and cons list made by the client.

In essence, so much conversation, nit-picking, evaluation and re-evaluation of the entire process boils down to four questions:

1. Did the agency team build the client's confidence?
2. Which finalist learned the most about the client team and the brand during the process?
3. Did the agency team leave the client team wanting more?
4. Can the client team imagine working with the agency team two to three years out…and see a positive ROI, as well as a successful relationship?

Clients don't just buy the creative concepts; they need to buy into the business solutions!

♥ **Pitching? Believe in the client's vision. Be open to their POV. Be one with their mission. Be sure to be truly interested. #newbusiness**

Strong strategy, data mining, and core consumer insights + a little Luck O'the Irish are needed for a new biz win. HSPD! #newbusiness

♥ **Tech issues during the pitch? Don't sweat! Stay calm and show you're in control. Clients want a collected group on their team! #newbusiness**

In the middle of the final pitch for a health insurance client, the agency's computer threw a wrench into the presentation. The application was frozen and the presenter couldn't advance to the next slide. She remained composed, kept speaking, "spoke in pictures" and allowed someone on the team to resolve the tech disaster in the background. All eyes were focused on her and not the computer problem. Was she dying inside? You bet! Did she show it? Not at all. During the debrief, one of the clients firmly stated, "When the sh*t hits the fan, I want this agency on my team!" Yes, they won the account.

Successful brands build para-social relationships. Try to create this phenomenon for your agency and stop pitching. #newbusiness

♥ **Final pitch? Solid strategy is vital connected to strong creative concepts but just make sure your brief isn't showing! :)** **#newbusiness**

Final Pitch prep question to ask the prospect: You would be disappointed after our pitch if we ___? #newbusiness

♥ **If the agency doesn't have the category experience be sure to highlight how the consumer experience is relevant and valuable. #newbusiness**

The pitch is a culmination of mtgs throughout the review process. The final pitch should leave the prospect wanting more! #newbusiness

Emotional appeal is an important part of the pitch. What needs are you trying to address & what emotions address those needs? #newbusiness

Focus on one meeting at a time (not the entire pitch process at once) with a "nothing to lose" attitude. #newbusiness

♥ **Answering an RFI? Tell the client what you're doing to ensure agency growth/innovative thinking (even if it's not a question). #newbusuness**

If you're going to share a story during a pitch meeting be sure to have a purpose. #newbusiness

♥ **At the end of a pitch process it comes down to two vital factors: talent and chemistry. #newbusiness**

Chemistry meeting? Be authentic, present as a cohesive team & have internal chemistry (even if you've recently met)! #newbusiness

Chemistry mtg tip: present as a cohesive team exemplifying internal chemistry (hint: you can't fake it)! #newbusiness

♥ **Simple pitch tip: keep the lights on when presenting! You're not in a theater. You're delivering valuable information. #newbusiness**

Don't let your nervousness override your passion when presenting. #newbusiness

Want a winning presentation? Be brief, novel, concrete and visual! #newbusiness

Successful presentations must do three things: inform, empower, engage (entertain). #newbusiness

♥ **Stories have stopping power because as humans we want to know what happens next. Add a relevant story to your pitch. #newbusiness**

It's not just what you say. It's how you say it! #newbusiness

Very short pitch presentation times with complex pitch assignments? Ditch the pitch! #newbusiness

If you truly know your material, you don't need PowerPoint. #newbusiness

Do more agencies win the pitch when pitching 1st or last? Content & cultural compatibility matter not order of the lineup. #newbusiness

♥ **A sure-fire way of disengaging your prospect within 5 seconds? Sticking to a script! #newbusiness**

Shock value with rationale has sticking power (otherwise it's undervalued). #newbusiness

♥ **Does the idea seem threatening? Don't run from it... #newbusiness**

Secret writing skill? Bring topics into the present. The reader will feel more engaged if they feel the experience is recent. #newbusiness

Pitching a new account? Don't forget to read and more importantly, RE-READ the client's brief before the pitch... #newbusiness

♥ **If you're speaking too fast, there's too much content crammed into the prez! The simpler you say it, the more eloquent it is! #newbusiness**

Need an unbiased creative critic for a pitch? Ask one of your current clients for their honest opinion. #newbusiness

♥ **The best credentials meetings are great chemistry meetings! #newbusiness**

Hindsight is 20/20. Foresight is infinite possibilities. Bring a mixture of both to every new biz pitch! #newbusiness

There's no real playbook. It's simply genuine, authentic passion! #newbusiness

Does the brief lack clarity? Request clarification. Don't start the process w/o being crystal clear of the client's needs. #newbusiness

Did the competition accidentally leave behind their materials in the pitch room? Don't let temptation take over...keep focus! #newbusiness

The heart trumps the head - 80% of our choices are emotional. #ANAMasters #newbusiness

♥ **Visual content is the key to driving emotional connections - it's a free pass to the emotional side of your brain. #ANAMasters #newbusiness**

Pitching? Bring the prospect the needle not the haystack! #newbusiness

♥ **Prove to your prospects that you believe in their mission, vision and beliefs not just in the product they're selling. #newbusiness**

It's not what you say. It's what they hear! #newbusiness

Charged w/ being the leader? It Doesn't Matter What You Know If You Can't Communicate

From the mouth of a marketer: the best creds mtgs are great chemistry mtgs!

♥ **Some of the most impactful presentations are conversations.**

Showing creative at final pitch? Consider validating the creative via consumer testing.

♥ **Pitching as the incumbent? Don't "sell your agency." Show how you've been an extension to the mktg team that moved the business!**

Are you speaking only to the silver hair in the room? Caution! It's often the junior person who has a heavy hand in the final decision.

♥ **Day to day team member can't make the chemistry mtg? Client interpretation: my biz isn't important enough for this agency!**

How do mktrs judge agencies? Strategic thinking anchored in innovative creative engaging consumers on multiple platforms (& chemistry counts)!

Presenting? Deliver an experience not just facts, figures and features.

Exemplify your process but don't appear to be "text-book oriented." Be human...

♥ **Lots of people in the prospective client meeting? Use name cards! #newbusiness**

If you have a pre-established relationship with 1 of the prospective clients in the mtg, don't fall victim to speaking mostly to that person.

♥ **You can't take anyone professionally if you can't take them personally. #newbusiness @BreneBrown #HOWLive**

Don't try to win the business in one meeting...focus on getting invited to the next one instead.

♥ **When pitching a new creative campaign be sure to show it on a mobile device! Mobile usage trumps TV time. #ForbesCMOSummit #newbusiness**

The power of big data is vital for deep insights but don't lose sight of the power of the big idea!

Pitching? Consider a 3-minute brand video. Show how you see the brand & talk top line thoughts on where you think the brand should go & why.

Pitching? Be sure to talk evolution and not revolution...show how you will evolve the prospect's current marcom plans (don't just dump 'em)!

No search consultant managing the review? Act like the consultant & offer evaluation guidelines & suggestions for a comprehensive process.

Don't be over aggressive...just get to the next mtg. "Let's talk," uses today's interaction to make it more likely you have one tomorrow.

♥ **Presenting with confidence not arrogance will help you to connect with your prospect. Speak in stories!**

Presenting is about connection – and you get that through sharing your passion, resonating w/people, & being authentic.

♥ **Self-deprecation serves well as the relationship progresses but can be interpreted as a lack of confidence as a first impression.**

2 ways to create an effective Super Bowl ad: use humor or tug at the heart strings. Include a touch of both for new biz pitches!

Don't have a POV? Don't expect to win the pitch!

Spontaneity takes a lot of preparation. Practice makes perfect but the talent of the speaker makes the audience believe it's off the cuff.

♥ **Add light humor in your presentation...it helps audiences relate to what you're trying to communicate.**

Chemistry mtg? Sit AT the table w/the prospective client (not off to the side)! Simple suggestion to immediately create warmth & chemistry.

♥ **Final pitch? Presenting idea after idea doesn't show your creativity. It shows lack of judgement regarding strategic business solutions!**

Tongue in cheek is ok once...after that it cheapens the brand!

Be the expert but don't appear as being narrow minded. Be sure to see & show all possibilities in the pitch process!

❤ **Prepping for chemistry mtg? Answer this question: The client should invite your agency to the next round because____? #newbusiness**

If you're asked to make a certain number of copies for the presentation...always add an extra (just in case)!

Writing a presentation? Use info-graphics to capture attention and drive vital points. Most people are visual!

The greatest brand stories play off of tension: Southwest, Apple, Target. Create tension in your communications AND presentations!

Writing an RFI? 3 - 5 case studies show experience and depth without being too overwhelming to read!

Uncomfortable ideas often expand comfort zones. But "walk before you run" and don't frighten the client with ideas that are too innovative!

❤ **Prepping for a final pitch? Mehrabian's formula for key presentation skills: 7% verbal, 38% vocal, 55% visual...YOU are the most important visual!**

Presenting creative? Don't forget to show how you analyze your own work and why you got to the final recommendation you made.

♥ **Clients typically decide against hiring an agency due to their lack of understanding re: the client's biz, category & the agency's value!**

Presenting creative? Great ideas also need excellent execution. Show both!

Presenting creative? Show insights to inspiration and make sure the insights are behavior led.

♥ **Laughter strengthens relationship bonds and regulates emotions in stressful situations. Add some humor to biz relationships. #newbusiness**

No search consultant managing the review? Act as one! Be organized, offer a schedule, suggest chemistry & tear sheet mtgs before the pitch!

Prepping for a final presentation? Be careful of choice overload. Transactional decisions happen more easily when there are less choices!

♥ **Don't be concerned with a "Goliath." Your competitor's biggest strength is often their greatest weakness.**

Be sure to present multiple ideas at a final presentation but it is vital to have a recommendation on one and a POV!

Agencies must form valuable partnerships with clients by understanding their business and challenging their internal thinking!

♥ **Pitching? Show you're ahead of the curve but don't be so far around the bend that the client feels they aren't ready for you! #newbusiness**

When managing a review for a B2B client, there was an agency in consideration that was on top of the category, showed innovative and futuristic thinking to help the brand stand out. Although the client appreciated such viewpoints, they knew it would be "too much to sell to executive management." With that said, they eliminated the agency from the process. Exemplifying that your agency is abreast of industry changes and trends is welcomed by marketers but be cautious of sounding overwhelming.

Crucial elements from the mktr perspective include the requirement that agencies understand exactly what a brand's values are in its mktg.

♥ **Pitching? Don't spend 20 min on an "understanding" not about the task at hand. You'll lose the prospect's attention & worse their interest.**

Pitching? Don't sell. Use examples to illustrate your thinking. Prospects should arrive at your conclusion before you do.

People read 4x faster than a speaker can speak. Control what the audience is looking at and make sure they're listening to you!

Incumbents typically start from a deeper hole than the "shiny new objects of desire" a pitch offers so be rational about defending!

♥ **Incumbent defending acct? Present new group & keep 1 person from prior team. Client has a new agency w/historical experience. #newbusiness**

Don't share too much info based only on preliminary research about the prospect you haven't met yet! It can be a slippery slope.

Remember, pitching a prospect isn't a 1-way street! The agency must evaluate the client just as much as the client must evaluate the agency.

♥ **Are you truly engaged in the meeting? Stop checking emails and texts and be respectful of everyone's time! #newbusiness**

Pitching? Risk being right. Don't play it safe but be smart. Relevancy has a deadline!

Be sure to remove the previous prospect's name in the RFI!! Sloppiness is an automatic reason for elimination.

Adding a screen shot to the doc? Make sure it's legible! Fuzzy dashboards that are unreadable with no explanation are useless!

♥ **Fight for the work you believe in but be sure it's a rational and not emotional debate! #newbusiness**

If the RFI doesn't request creative reel/portfolio - DON'T provide it! It's too easy to start judging creative which is all too subjective!

What wins the pitch? It's a step by step relationship-building approach from the first conversation!

♥ **Agency growth shouldn't always be a primary goal. Agency health first. Love who you're pitching; be selective. #newbusiness #AASmallAgency**

Present ideas that are intrusive without quick wear out!

Show the power behind the big idea...and execution counts!

Bake in analytics from the start. Don't show it as a standalone tactic. Show how it builds the brand!

♥ **Breaking rules can help you to stand out but know the boundaries before you color outside the lines. #newbusiness**

Less words! Use more bullets and visuals that tell the story. Too many pages of type-heavy layout lose the reader's attention faster.

When writing an RFI do a bit of research about the prospective client and leave them asking for more!

Detail what each case study demonstrates! Problem solved, Insights learned, Solutions offered and Results received.

Write an impactful case study by exemplifying the relevance to the prospective client!

♥ **Simple pitch tip: repeat the assignment in your final pitch presentation so everyone is on the same page. #newbusiness**

Final Presentation? Focus on creative ideas anchored in strategy! Pitch theater is distracting and detracts from the content.

♥ **Final pitch question: Did you leave the prospective client with the confidence they want to offer you their business? #newbusiness**

Exemplify creative width (more than depth) in order to show the client that you can interpret the strategy in multiple ways.

If it's not your turn to speak, sit down or stand "off stage." Too many people just standing idle while one is presenting is distracting!

Intimately know your content without being scripted. Relax and allow yourself to connect with the audience.

♥ **You can't always control the results. But you own your efforts, your ideas, and your perseverance. Be positive and authentic. #newbusiness**

Shared values and interests are a far more powerful aggregator of human beings than demographic categories alone...find the shared interests

Boredom sets in fast! Have a hook in the opening seconds. Creating emotional rollercoasters (terminate joy then restore it) generates suspense and thereby keeping prospects wanting more.

♥ **What's requested and what's expected are sometimes not in sync. Listen carefully and read between the lines! #newbusiness**

The element of surprise is what helps prospects to remember...but surprise, not shock, evokes joy which is what sticks.

Want to exemplify passion for the prospect's business? Don't have too many people in the room!

♥ **Do not highlight agency awards! It is a turn off to clients. Talk business results linked to communications strategy.**

Using PowerPoint? Short bullet points are good; headline only is better; images only are best!

Show entertainment value LINKED to a core idea, authentic principle & higher order benefit articulating brand purpose around share values!

Are you the owner of the agency? The CEO? The global CMO? Be sure to LEAD your group in meetings. Do NOT dominate!

Want to talk about agency process? Be sure to highlight the PEOPLE, their talent and relevant experience behind that process!

♥ **Remember that the "how" in what you say is often more important than the "what!" #newbusiness**

What to get out of a work session from the prospect? Consolidated feedback from the ENTIRE mktg team. Show that you're listening to EVERYONE.

♥ **One of the keys to success: make it memorable! Even if you make a flop - acknowledge it, lighten the moment & make it unique. #newbusiness**

Using humor? Balance it out with more serious strategic thinking. Exemplify both sides.

Writing an RFI? Commodity brands that have gone to another level emotionally typically get noticed. Starbucks vs. Maxwell House.

If the "theater" isn't relevant to the presentation...don't do it!

❤ **When a prospect agrees with you on a point, let it stand. Don't prolong the conversation. Give them time to think about why they agree w/you.**

Presenting 1st, 2nd or last? It doesn't matter! Nothing trumps pure passion and innovative thinking.

Using humor in presentations? Proceed with caution. What's funny to you can be offensive to others. Avoid inside jokes.

Winning pitch pointers? Match client tone on a human level. Listen first. Be authentic.

Defending the account? Play offense NOT defense! Be hungry, show passion, rekindle the relationship.

❤ **Need category experience? People, not agencies, have the sector experience. #newbusiness**

Writing an RFI? Be sure the prospect can read it! If not, they lose interest. Hint: dark, normal size font, white space, light background.

Prepping for a final pitch? Speak to the depths of the brand & be sure to highlight deep emotional motivators.

Lose the "agency speak." Storytelling captures the essence of what it means to be human.

♥ **Create value not novelty! #newbusiness**

How do you know if you're the "dark horse"? ASK! Probe. Find out why you were invited to pitch?

♥ **You'll never learn anything while you're talking! #newbusiness**

Work Session? Engage the client in discussion. Don't speak at them. Speak w/them. Show them what it's like to work with the agency team!

Prepping for a final pitch? Demonstrate desire; bring ideas to life with visuals; have a stake in the ground.

♥ **Selecting the final agency can literally come down to "who would you rather have a beer with" when all else is completely comparable!**

Prepping for a final pitch? Open with 10 minutes of reinstating relevant experience, proof points and reasons why the agency is a finalist!

Marketers want proof points to exemplify that you will deliver on your promise!

## Passionate Pitching? Make sure there's real substance behind the "stunt"... otherwise, don't do it!

I've watched many theater-like presentations and quite a few pitch-schtick stunts over the years. This one was for a well-known ice cream brand. We got to Philadelphia's 30th Street Station with the clients at about 11AM. Rush hour was over but the station was filled with people and many of them were eating from the newly launched ice cream mini cups. Coincidence? Not a shot but a nice touch. The problem? It didn't stop there. As we piled into cars for the 10 minute drive through the city to the agency, there were people dressed in cow costumes on the phone or reading the paper at certain locations. When we got to the agency, there was a real cow standing on sod, being milked as we entered the agency's front door. What did the client say? "They have no regard for their budget and I won't trust them with mine!"

♥ **Non-attendance of client top execs during the agency search? Think twice about pitching! #newbusiness**

Take advantage of work sessions! Communicate goals; clarify expectations, detail research & strategic thinking before talking creative.

♥ **Keep the prospect engaged by having energy in the room! If you're not exemplifying passion then how can they be passionate about you!?**

Prepping for a chemistry mtg? Reread the RFI and be sure to exemplify expertise on key objectives detailed on the RFI.

♥ **Writing an RFI? Reinforce the major ideas you want to be remembered! Highlight the main "take-away" since the client is reading MANY RFI's!**

David v. Goliath in a pitch? Exemplify your leadership, speed, innovation, flexibility, focus and value-based costs!

Prepping for a chemistry mtg? Provide a sheet containing photos of folks on the proposed team with their names and titles!

Prepping for a chemistry meeting? Executive mgmt should NEVER monopolize the meeting and EVERYONE in the room should have a speaking role!

Writing an RFI? Don't use technical jargon or acronyms that mean nothing to the prospect!

♥ **Preparing a presentation? Apply the 666 rule: no more than 6 words per bullet, 6 bullets per image, 6 word slides in a row.**

Pitching? Confidence (not arrogance) is alluring. Jumping through hoops exemplifies desperation...show that you're in control!

♥ **100+ page response for an RFI? Really? Brevity = Clarity = Relevance!**

High Tech vs. High Touch: Effective presenters use high-touch elements and the presenter is an integral part of the presentation.

♥ **Preparing a presentation? We see presentations, we don't read them. Use effective imagery to be more engaging. Vision trumps all senses.**

♥ **Preparing a presentation? What colors should you use? Blue is calming, yellow is for optimism, red stirs excitement and can agitate.**

How to lose a pitch: not showing the analytics and measurement plan behind evaluating the communications plan.

♥ **How to lose a pitch: failure to build the relationship and chemistry by not demonstrating how you truly want to help their business.**

Pitch to win. Don't pitch to pitch. Be selective with rational reasons!

The definition of results can be different between agency & client. If you're exemplifying category expertise, use their lexicon, not yours!

♥ **An innovative pitch idea is only 50% of the battle. Successful execution is the other 50%...communicate, meet deadlines, do what you say!**

Four vital I's in new biz: inform, invite, include, interact. Reminder: Pitch to win. Don't pitch just to pitch! Be selective and sincere.

The majority of incumbents don't keep the business. Can you increase your chances? Reignite the passion and creativity by changing the team!

♥ **Vital questions mktrs keep in mind while searching for an agency? What makes you...well, you? What's your avg employee tenure? #newbusiness**

Total Integration = Category, Consumer, Brand and Business insights talking the same language at every touch point.

What do clients think about creative being presented: Is the creative presented too complicated or too sophisticated for our consumers?

Shift the focus from "price" to "value of services" and show how you offer insights innovation to your prospects' problems.

Doing an agency tour? Don't walk aimlessly through the agency. Tell a story, express your culture, exemplify your talent.

♥ **A sure-fire way to lose the pitch? Concentrating on agency capabilities and not on the client's specific business objectives. #newbusiness**

Being unique has no value in itself...capture the essence of your identity in words and images.

Don't try to win the business in the first conversation. Develop the 3Cs: chemistry, conversation and cultural connections.

♥ **Writing an RFI? Know who's reading it! Who's involved in decisions? Is procurement involved? Then be sure to be focused on VALUE!**

Should you show one creative execution when pitching for business? Only if you're pitching against yourself!

❤ **Marketers' reason to disqualify an agency in consideration? "They think they can address our needs w/little client input." #newbusiness**

Mktrs are less interested in isolated creative ideas—they need strategy, process, and broad thinking to get to a business solution.

In today's hyper social-networked world, the strategy is often the big idea.

What do clients want to see from a potential agency partner? Aspiration, Passion and a sense of Urgency about their business!

❤ **A client concern during the review process? "I want to be guaranteed that the team I meet is the team I get!" #newbusiness**

Clients' concern when selecting an agency: "Can I go to war with them and will the agency team stand tall through the fight ahead?"

Do you have a star player on your presentation team? Don't let him overpower the rest. Clients' concern: what if he leaves the team?

❤ **What do mktrs want in an RFI? Personalization without the overkill of poor assumptions. #newbusiness**

What do clients think about when evaluating creative concepts? Is it "ownable," "sellable" and emotional w/legs!

Client rationale for agency selection: "Insightful and integrated team with intellectual depth regarding our category and consumer!"

Anchor strategy in research; anchor creative in strategy and be sure the message creates resonance!

♥ **Do you firmly believe in your idea? Defend it but don't die on your sword! Exemplify flexibility & listening skills!**

Pitching a prospective client? 1. Be detailed in your strategic thinking. 2. Show creative ideas...don't bank on just one!

Preparing for a chemistry meeting w/a prospect? Too many people in the room will KILL the chemistry...team who is day-to-day only!

♥ **Pitching? Presentations aren't about the most concise exposition of facts, they are about changing minds. #newbusiness**

Preparing for a chemistry meeting with a potential client? Be genuine. Show relevant experience. Don't seem contrived!

Chemistry is vital when considering a new business partner but it doesn't trump business insights and smarts!

♥ **Preparing for a chemistry meeting? Marketers look for pro-active thought leadership.**

## Writing an RFI? PLEASE PLEASE spell check! Especially the client's name!!

I've read hundreds and hundreds of RFIs during my career as a search consultant and more often than not typos creep into the submissions. Many clients pick up on them. Some have some slight tolerance but most do not. During an agency review for Lindblad Expeditions, the client passed on a specific RFI without ever reading beyond the cover page. Why? The name of the company isn't Lindbald! It's LindBLAD! It was a heart-breaker since that RFI was right in line with the client's criteria. Every submission must be proof read a minimum of three times by three different readers.

## ♥ Client concern when conducting an agency search: "How will the agency keep the momentum/excitement going 3 to 5 yrs from now?" #newbusiness

Communicate something significant with conviction!

Sell dreams not services and develop creative ideas that aren't ads!

Top Lead Generation Error: Spending on marketing activities that are "vanity exercises" (i.e. excessive graphic design).

How to lose a pitch: failure to listen; didn't do your HW; all about me; creative/strategic disconnect; didn't build the chemistry!

Substance, content and insights will always win over non-strategic theater and drama in a presentation. Be yourself and be sincere.

High tech presentations can be fascinating but high touch is engaging! Being informal can form stronger bonds.

♥ **Writing an RFI? Be concise, show relevant work that resonates, leave them wanting more - share relevant trends about the category & consumer.**

Presenting first or last? It doesn't matter! Worry about "what" NOT "when"!

♥ **It's not just about the people but the TEAM. It's not just about the winning but the MANNER. #newbusiness**

Talk about failures as long as you learned from them what you learned is relevant to the prospects' biz. Success is failure inside out!

Use numbers from your research and tell a story. Be sure to keep it simple.

♥ **Client thinking in work session: push me to the point of discomfort in order to help my brand disrupt the category.**

Prospects usually don't remember your agency philosophy or creds. They do remember if you taught them something that will impact their biz!

Time is valuable and creative thought is even more so don't undervalue either!

Failure to prepare is preparing to fail... rehearse, rehearse and yes...rehearse again.

♥ **Posting content as part of your prospecting strategy? Don't post anything unless you deem it worthy of paying to distribute. #newbusiness**

Dig Deeper! Don't accept the first answer you get. Ask follow-up questions to get more detail and surface the real story!

♥ **Happy Fourth of the July! Why are fireworks so engaging? It's the element of surprise. Add a little of it to presentations and watch things spark! #newbusiness**

It's not about rules...it's about possibilities!

1 piece of political advice works in business, too...if you're in the lead, don't debate the challenger!

♥ **Be sure the experience exceeds the expectations when pitching new clients! #newbusiness**

Pitching a new client? Saying what you don't do is just as important as knowing what you will do...and you'll be more successful too!

K. Witsil, Chase Credit Cards: marketers must have a clear objective for an agency review; agencies must be honest regarding capabilities.

Pitching a new client? Be sure NOT to stop at communications rationale...tie EVERYTHING to business ROI!

More choices often lead to disappointment. Simplicity is the key to powerful ideas and attracting evangelists.

Does the client REALLY want to buy cutting edge work? The counter-culture approach seldom works. Ask questions to validate their requests.

♥ **Pitching? Remember the rule of 3 (3 key messages can only be retained in short term memory) within 18 minutes or less. #newbusiness**

Deciding to defend a current account that's up for review? The average is a 1/20 chance of retaining. Think before you defend.

Pipe down and LISTEN! A vital skill that's often ignored. Don't finish sentences...you deny yourself potential positive outcomes.

Studies show that audiences remember 30% or less of presentation content. Remember 3 keys to increase recall: Inform, Entertain, Inspire.

Spent 2 days touring ad agencies the best comment made was not about capabilities but more about compassion. "We sell comfort to clients!"

♥ **Listen to what you say and how you say it. That's typically how a prospective client determines if "you get them." #newbusiness**

80% of buyers experience at least 1 major problem during a professional services purchase. #1 problem: didn't listen to me!

Marketers are expected to do more with less! Be respectful of their time. Be business-focused, not product-centric.

♥ Be sure to address the junior clients in the room...they "grow up" fast & often have more say in the decision that you think! #newbusiness

Don't tell clients that your agency has social expertise...show it!

If you find yourself addressing clients' needs with cynicism...be still and don't speak. Truly listen to their thoughts and outlook first.

♥ Setting sensible boundaries help you to become more valuable. When you're more valuable people wait for your contribution. #newbusiness

Do you have women in the room? Clients notice (especially when it's a team of mostly female marketers)!

Pitch tips from marketers: be on the same page; COMMUNICATE; brevity is vital; LISTEN; be authentic, chemistry is vital, be a partner!

♥ Pitching? Remember you're a TEAM! Together Everybody Achieves More. #newbusiness

90% of information transmitted to the brain is visual and visuals are processed 60k times faster in the brain than text.

♥ "Creative Vomit" is the best way to lose a pitch! 3 creative concepts...TOPS with a recommended direction. #newbusiness

**♥ Puh-leeease…stop texting during meetings! Leave your cell phone on your desk and go mobile-free. #newbusiness**

Unfortunately, we're a society addicted to technology and worse, addicted to our smartphones. Of course, there are many great benefits that have come with technology but also some real issues. The problem with using your smartphone during a meeting is the dilemma of perception versus reality. During a chemistry meeting for a multi-million dollar account, the CMO of the agency pulled out his phone to send a text message. After the meeting, the prospective client instantly eliminated them from the search for a few reasons with the primary one being texting during the meeting. However, what the client didn't know was that the CMO of the agency was texting his assistant to bring more coffee into the meeting! Perception versus reality can be a really big deal breaker… and one hell of an expensive text.

**♥ No category experience & the agency is still a finalist. Why? Authentic, integrated team that made non-category work relevant!**

Agency size larger than size criteria but still a finalist. Why? Passionate/authentic team, solutions oriented, tradigital thinking displayed!

## PART IV: POST PITCH PURSUITS

♥ **"Good relationships don't just happen. They take time, patience, and people who truly want to be together." ~Unknown**

I'm always thrilled when I get to call the agency that won the account after an arduous pitch process but I often chuckle and say, "I have good news and bad news. The good news is you won the account. The bad news is you won the account." Client/agency relationships – just like personal relationships – are a mix of good and bad, ups and downs.

Nevertheless, it's always exciting to begin a new relationship. There's the thrill of getting to know someone new and discovering new things together, experiencing the "x-factor" (that special something that triggers chemistry), and incorporating this relationship into your life. And there are many similar experiences in a new client relationship – the thrill of the win; the chemistry with a new team; the sigh of relief that the pitch investment wasn't all for naught; and of course, smoothly onboarding the client.

♥ **Fortitude and partnership should always be built into the agency relationship as part of the compensation plan.**

But like any relationship, the bloom can fall off the rose; the newness can become ordinary and partners can become complacent. I remember managing a home-office equipment agency review for an exciting project on which all the agencies involved truly wanted to work. It was a great product, an interesting assignment and a well-known brand. During the chemistry meetings, the SVP of marketing asked a very interesting question of all finalists: "How does the agency continue to keep the momentum, passion and ideals (not just ideas) alive after the honeymoon is over?" The best response I heard dealt with selecting an agency that has a similar business philosophy and that believes in the client's mission and vision – not just in the product being sold. Sharing in the vision and drive for the brand also tied into their compensation arrangement.

♥ **Although we live in a world of instant gratification, ironically, gratifying relationships are not built instantly. #newbusiness**

Business relationships are analogous to personal relationships in so many ways. There are innumerable books, articles, blogs and more all offering ridiculous amounts of relationship advice but I believe successful relationships (whether they are personal or business) boil down to three key actions: make quality time; keep constant communication; show small acts of kindness by putting the other person first.

**Make quality time.** I don't mean just having weekly status calls. Everyone involved on the account should spend time with the client team outside the office. Lunches, dinners, drinks are all good, but it's more than breaking bread. Make time for a two-day retreat or an out-of-office outing. Learn what makes each person on both sides of the team happy or worried; get to know their personal philosophies; understand their personal passions. It's the *people* that make relationships thrive – or drive them into the ground.

**Keep constant communication.** We're in the business of communications and yet we often fail at communicating! Talk about everything – the good, the bad and the ugly. The successful agency relationship is one that becomes an extension of the client marketing team and that only happens when there is continuous contact and communication.

**Show small acts of kindness.** As I stated, it's not uncommon to hear from clients that the agency has become complacent or doesn't worry about my business the way I do. Small acts of kindness means staying on top of the competitive set; knowing what's coming next in the (social) media world; thinking about ideas to help innovate the brand; and offering your point of view consistently to show that you authentically care and are passionate about the brand, the client's success and your relationship year after year after year.

Cultivating relationships isn't easy and maintaining them is harder. New business efforts do not end when you're celebrating a win. In fact, it's just the beginning. It is hard work to be married, but it's more difficult and painful to get divorced so be sure to be committed to the key rules for maintaining strong client relationships: keep the lines of communication open and healthy, and always treat your current clients like prospects!

The fortune is in the details.

Incumbent who lost? Be classy. Set up a transition meeting w/ client and new agency. #newbusiness

❤ **If your agency is ending a relationship, be sure to end on a high note & complete all biz until the contract officially ends. #newbusiness**

Put a value on outcome instead of a price on time input. #newbusiness

Creating a compensation proposal? Charge for intellectual capital instead of capacity. #newbusiness

Agencies that create value define predictive modeling. #newbusiness

Agency materials must be distinctive, emotive, and integrated in order to be memorable. #newbusiness

❤ **Don't know the client's budget? Don't pitch. #newbusiness**

Align economic interests with those of the prospective client and create a tailored comp proposal. #newbusiness

New clients coming on board? Call a review before they do and show your value! #newbusiness

❤ **Always define hard and soft metrics of success to demonstrate accountability. #newbusiness**

Be sure your leave-behind includes clear contact info, photos and short bios of key team members. Clients hire people! #newbusiness

Offer a free two week ramp up period as part of your comp proposal and show you have skin in the game. #newbusiness

**♥ Clients are concerned with bait and switch. Have a Pitch Team Warranty to guarantee they get who they meet during the pitch. #newbusiness**

I haven't met a client search committee yet who isn't concerned with meeting the "pitch team" and not the day-to-day team responsible for their account should the agency win their business. A chemistry meeting or work session should never end without the agency team confirming whom on their team gets the call from the client…and that person should be vocal in the meeting! I can recall a huge financial review that AAR managed where the lead account person didn't say two words during the meeting and when the question popped up as to who should be the person to receive that first call from the client, guess who raised his hand? Needless to say, it was the wrong answer! The agency team must guarantee that the senior team in the room is responsible for the account and is not just a pitch team.

Creating a comp proposal? Don't charge for executive time! Put it in the overhead and waive some hours. #newbusiness

**♥ Keep printed leave-behinds concise and leave the details on the memory stick! #newbusiness**

New biz 101: treat your clients like prospects. #newbusiness

❤ **Don't become complacent. Keep the spark alive with your current client relationships! #newbusiness**

Does the senior most acct exec only reach out to the client when there's a problem or good news to share? If so, make a change. #newbusiness

❤ **Relationship issues creeping in? Have a "dinnervention." Make a reservation and have dinner with your client. Talk face to face.**

If you want to go fast, go along with it. If you want to go far, go together! Be a TEAM with your client group. #newbusiness

Maybe you lost the pitch but you developed a relationship. Steward it. Nurture it. Leverage it. People move & make referrals. #newbusiness

Address needs and desires but also anticipate where change may (and should) occur. #newbusiness

❤ **Remember it's not so much B2C or B2B as it is P2P (person to person). We're in the biz of relationships! #newbusiness**

The best mtgs are when you help mktrs think about something they never thought of before for their brand. Be sure to pleasantly surprise...

Successful stewardship means set expectations and then deliver beyond those expectations...every single time!

Magic, anticipation, good cheer...a little bit of the Christmas spirit should be added to every new biz pitch throughout the year!

Negotiating? If you're not willing to walk away, you can't negotiate an equitable and effective plan.

Negotiating? We all like pleasant human interactions but remember that negotiators often inflate their emotions hoping you will concede.

How to get the most out of your client relationship? Establish clear expectations on scope and responsibility. Schedule regular assessments!

♥ **Want a stand-out leave-behind? Include relevant POVs and usable insights based on data. #newbusiness**

Are you too proficient? A well-oiled machine churns out clone after clone. Be efficient but not at the price of sacrificing effectiveness!

♥ **Outstanding leadership is a resonant relationship...are you in sync with your relationships in order to create productivity? #newbusiness**

Clients are hiring YOU! Be memorable, informative & sincere. Have an engaging leave-behind that HIGHLIGHTS vital presentation points!

Want a powerful connection with procurement? Align payment and reward to drive desired behaviors and value delivery.

You get what you pay for! Commoditizing talent based services will only increase the risk to your business!

Breakthrough RFPs? Low Core Fee + Sweat Equity Investment + Performance Based Revenue

**♥ Lost the pitch? Continue sharing thought leadership content and show authentic interest for the next opportunity. #newbusiness**

Creating a compensation plan? People, brainpower and talents are not a commodity! Don't devalue your services.

How to get the most out of your client relationship? Request a well-written, effective brief and continual updated info from the client POV.

An agency staffing plan is more than a semblance for required tasks...evaluate the contribution of strategic and tactical staff.

Shift the focus from "price" to "value of services" and show how you offer insights & innovation to your prospects' problems.

Exemplify the perceived emotional value more than financial investment.

**♥ Lesson #1: Spell check all leave-behind agency collateral material. #newbusiness**

The greatest indication of true interest is giving time! Give time to your current clients, as well as your prospects!

❤ **Lost the pitch? Write a sincere thank you note anyway. #newbusiness**

Hand-written thank you notes seem to be a thing of the past but there are two words that are strong relationship-builders: thank you. The deliberation meetings after all final presentations have concluded can be mentally exhausting. The conversations, questions, concerns, and debates that happen behind closed doors can go on for hours as the marketing team tries to make the most comprehensive and insightful final selection. And quite often the decision is almost the flip of a coin between two agencies. In fact there was a review where the final decision was at a complete deadlock. The marketing team could not make the decision and instead agreed to sleep on the final two agencies and regroup in 24-hours. Within that time frame, one of the two agencies had a hand-written note delivered to each person on the marketing team. That thank you note became the tie-breaker and the agency was awarded the account. Win, lose or draw...write a thank you note (hint: write it before the final selection is made!).

Developing a leave-behind? Make sure it's cryptic until you've brought it to life with explanation.

Are you offering value exchange!?!

Be sure to explain why you can't provide great service and a great product AND have the best price in your market.

❤ **Metrics should be established as incremental and not all or nothing. #newbusiness**

The Net Promoter Ultimate Question to always keep in mind: How likely are you to recommend our product to your friends on a scale of 1-10?

The best negotiators walk shoulder-to-shoulder instead of being confrontational face-to-face.

♥ **Think about ditching time sheets and bill on value instead. #newbusiness**

In the game of charging less, we often under deliver too...show the VALUE of what your services are worth (and OVER deliver instead)!

Negotiating for a better deal? Don't negotiate your way into poor service lack of talent. Remember, we all get what we pay for in the end.

Retention? Consider diversification re-envisioning current skills/products...helps reach new markets keep existing clients' attention.

♥ **Agencies must shift the perspective from being an expenditure to an investment. #newbusiness**

Want to avoid dickering about fees? Effectively communicate the value of the service you provide!

Cutting prices for prospects? May be interpreted as a sign of the agency in trouble. Slashing prices could prove costly in the long run!

Annual reviews. Hated by managers & employees; ignored the rest of the year. Give immediate mgmt feedback when employees excel/fall short.

♥ **Always be thankful for all your relationships. Show grace and gratitude each and every day. Happy Thanksgiving. #newbusiness**

Offer discounts? This alters the prospect's attitude who now believes the real value of the service is the reduced price not the full one.

Almost 30% of CFOs view marketing initiatives as a high cost or "a waste." Agencies MUST show the ROI and always prove their VALUE!

It's easy to forget that making money and making friends can go hand-in-hand in business. Build your business by building relationships!

The definition of "value" in a recession is a ?. Are you costing your clients more this year, or even this quarter, than you will save them?

♥ **Great creative wins new accounts. Outstanding account service keeps them. #newbusiness**

Show true partnership and share the burden on being cost-efficient...continuously. #newbusiness

Similar alternatives are what forces IP to be given at below value. Become a distinctive expert & get compensated fairly. #newbusiness

Friction can forge deeper partnerships as long as both teams LISTEN to both sides!

**Lost a review? You also built a relationship. KIT. People move. Things change. #newbusiness**

No one wants to lose a pitch, especially when your agency is one of three finalists. You're so close and yet not everyone can win the business. AAR Partners has lost pitches as well (yes, search consultants do pitch!) and it's absolutely heart-breaking at times. But there is a positive in all situations, and the silver lining in this one is the fact that you've built some rather solid relationships during the pitch process. And unless your team had a complete meltdown during the final presentation, typically you don't really lose…you just didn't win (I know, another tough line to swallow). When AAR Partners was involved with managing a casual dining review, the agency that lost really should have won, but didn't for a few, let's say, "political issues." Our advice to them was to continue fostering the relationship with the marketer, share helpful insights and information and don't let go. They took the advice and one year later, the account shifted to the "runner up" without a review. Better yet, they maintained a great relationship with the client for quite a few years.

♥ **Easter represents new life. Bring a bit a "new beginnings" into every client relationship each day and watch results soar. #newbusiness**

Think in terms of marketing partnerships not campaigns.

♥ **Did a current client move to a new company? Offer to help them on-board at no fee. #newbusiness**

A CMO's responsibility is more than just a chief marketing officer. Help them to be a Chief Motivating Officer with all brand ambassadors!

Help CMOs be the custodian of the brand in all areas & among all constituencies (customers, employees, media, regulators) view the brand

♥ **Show true partnership and waive some on-boarding hours for a new client. #newbusiness**

Client comp concerns? No transparency - implement open book policy for clients. #newbusiness

Good comp proposals need to detail expected results within specific time frames. #newbusiness

Thanksgiving is a day of sharing & caring w/o expecting anything in return. Carry this into everyday relationships w/clients. #newbusiness

♥ **Detail why you want to work on their business in your creds presentation. Make your mtg about them! #newbusiness**

Create a value compensation plan: define output rather than inputs. #newbusiness

Agree on the definition of value. Different definitions will lead to pressure on agency compensation. #newbusiness

The client/agency relationship needs a mix of historians who know the brands' past and new talent to challenge the future.

Client-Agency relationships must be committed to the BRAND. Not trying to impress the new CMO. Not always trying to find the new hot agency.

Don't sit idle. Be a change agent who creates new brand experiences, encourages innovative thinking and uses technology as an advantage.

❤ **Price your services on value and be sure you have a method for establishing/measuring the value you add.**

Thrive rather than survive during turbulent times. 1) Treat your clients like prospects and your prospects like clients. 2) Don't tell, sell!

❤ **Agencies must shift their compensation proposals from cost or time-based to value-based pricing. #newbusiness**

Do everything you can to win new business but don't do anything...your intellectual property is valuable!

Agency size smaller than size criteria but still a finalist. Why? Understood the brand, category and left the client with wanting more!

**Be sure to replace an outgoing agency team member on an account with someone who is just as competent (if not more). #newbusiness**

I received a call from a QSR client who was quite happy with their agency for seven years. Sales were up, creative was great, the strategy was strong...but they needed to call a review. Why? The agency replaced a critical and senior account person with someone who was too junior. The agency was also in flux with staffing changes and no one was paying attention. Unfortunately, it cost them the business.

## PART V: NURTURING AGENCY ASSETS

♥ **Agencies without a distinct position will forever be re-branding their agency. Put a stake in the ground!**

According to Shakespeare, a rose by any other name would smell as sweet. Although Juliet didn't give a hoot about Romeo's last name, in the business world, your name means everything. It precedes you. It defines you. It's your single greatest asset. Your agency's people may be the one and only proprietary tool but, unfortunately, they can be poached. Your name can never be taken from you and it must be protected. That means your emails, voicemails, presentations, fact sheets, credentials decks, RFIs, websites and social media all have your name on it in one form or another and must represent it well. They're all a reflection of YOU, and for boutique agencies that could mean your personal name, as well as the agency's name.

♥ **No point of differentiation = no interest. If you try to appeal to everyone, you'll gain the interest of no one. #newbusiness**

I sit through hundreds of agency credentials meetings every year, and to be very frank, most blend into each other. Try this little exercise in your office: cover the agency logo on different agency websites (if you can't get your hands on competitors' creds) and try to tell which one belongs to which agency. I bet you can't. Yet agencies talk about their mission, vision and processes as if they are unique. Having done this work for many years, I can tell you that very few truly are distinctive. I'm not saying that it's a snap to carve out what's specific to your agency and highlight distinguishable differences in a sentence or two. In fact, it's very difficult. However, those agencies with solid assets have painstakingly crafted their distinctions and their reason for being.

Those distinguishable differences?

1. Internalize what your agency is about…why does it exist?
2. Crystallize how you see the agency.
3. Know exactly what you're good at and why.
4. Stand for something and not everything.

Let's take a step back for a moment. I often get invited to lunch by new business executives in order to "pick my brain" on what the perception in the industry is of their agency.

This has always reminded me of the quote, "When you're 20, you care what everyone thinks; when you're 40, you stop caring what everyone thinks; when you're 60, you realize no one was ever thinking about you in the first place."

♥ **Your name means everything…especially when it comes to doing good business. Build a great name and always protect it by doing good first!**

And that goes for marketers thinking about agencies. Very few, if any, are thinking about your agency – or any other agency for that matter – on a daily basis. If they had to keep up with the agency landscape, they wouldn't be able to do their day job. They only think about agencies when they're in need of a new agency and then they hire a search consultant, ask for referrals from trusted sources, or do their own research. And all options bring me back to your name as being your greatest agency asset. Let your name speak for itself and make sure it can't be easily transferred to another agency that offers something similar. Define your "why" clearly, under promise and over deliver, and show why no one can replace you easily.

Client relationship consistently negative (unnecessary work; incompetent client lead)? Sever ties and boost internal morale. #newbusiness

React, adapt, communicate. Lessons of improv to apply to new business. #newbusiness

Don't be afraid to evaluate your clients and part ways with those who tax your team both monetarily and emotionally. #newbusiness

♥ **Are you the President or CEO? Let your team speak without talking on top of them. Show you trust them and their expertise!**

During an agency review for a non-governmental organization, there was a particular work session where the CEO of the agency expressed that he would leave the room for a few minutes to allow the team to carry on the conversation with the prospect. The client not only appreciated the fact that the CEO told them that he was going to leave the meeting for a short while to allow his team to continue the session, but they also interpreted it as one of trust with his team. He was engaged in the meeting but didn't monopolize it and showed a sense of respect and confidence with his team.

Labor Day pays tribute to the contributions of USA workers. Remember to celebrate your individual achievements made each day. #newbusiness

Need ideas for an "About Us" page on your agency's website that connects w/clients? http://blog.hubspot.com/agency/about-pages … #newbusiness

Want ideas? Look at start-ups & the tech world. That's where best ideas are generated/germinated. Let them guide your efforts. #newbusiness

There's a mix between knowing the data and knowing your brand but also trusting your intuition on a big creative idea. #newbusiness

Don't invest in ideas. Invest in people. #newbusiness

♥ **Creativity is the ultimate integration tool. #newbusiness @ BreneBrown #HOWLive**

Success is failures inside out. Make mistakes, learn from them and use it to win new biz! #newbusiness

Every so often just take a break...and let your mind absorb the tranquility. #newbusiness

Show the way it's "always been done" and juxtapose it against the way it could be done...highlight your innovation skills! #newbusiness

Efficiency vs Meaningful Tasks? In our knowledge-based economy, meaningful tasks creates ownership & increases productivity. #newbusiness

♥ **Think about brand purpose but think even more about your legacy...how you spend your time and with whom. #ANAMasters #newbusiness**

Purpose is too small of a word. Instead it's about ambitious purpose - a deep feeling about changing something. #ANAMasters

Would you hire your agency? Would you hire you? Why? #newbusiness

The best big business solutions are entrepreneurial at its core. #newbusiness

Pushing back on change? Don't. Find the benefits you will reap instead of fighting to keep the status quo. #newbusiness

If you have the "negative" spotlight on you for a moment, be sure to step up, share something positive and valuable. #newbusiness

Believing in your work is not a tactic! #newbusiness

♥ **Without trust there's nothing.**

"You can measure our agency by clients we don't have." M. Puris. In other words, be sure to stand for something...not everything! #smAARt

Treat ALL agency folks as "principals" since it is your people that differentiate your agency.

After all is said and done, more is typically said than done. Don't be that agency. Always over deliver!

By duplicating other biz models, we add layers of complexity to organizations that blur focus and erode profits.

❤ **In order to start a movement, true leaders embrace their followers as equals so that it's about the movement and not the leader.**

When you compassionately invite people to share their problems & you exemplify real-time solutions, you become the center of attraction.

There's a vital difference between depending on each other & becoming co-dependent. Being co-dependent = jumping through unnecessary hoops.

What does your agency video say about you? Too long: can't craft a story; No USP: can't identify a core insight; Lacks results: no impact.

Want to be invaluable to your clients? Become their community manager...understand the local nuances and how it impacts their brand.

❤ **Most of what we do gets rejected. You just need the GRIT to get to great. #newbusiness #AASmallAgency**

Need to produce an agency "culture" video? Show the spirit of the agency & philosophical commitment to clients that will impact their ROI!

When you don't make mistakes, you're not being innovative! (But remember to share the lesson learned from the failure).

Starting a new agency? 3 keys include: Digitally-centric thinking, deep data with insights, and the best talent money can buy!

❤ **Creative minds will always trump bells & whistles of tech & remain a driving force behind great ads (no matter what or how the biz changes).**

Advertising is an art but it must be a science of metrics every single day.

Don't demotivate your talent...be selective in new biz opportunities!

The new medium is: the human experience.

Vision, discipline, passion and moral conscience...the vital traits behind extraordinary accomplishments!

Great leaders make everyone feel comfortable at sharing their thoughts and ideas!

The most successful businesses speak to and engage people...they don't target consumers!

Successful change is almost always specific, not general.

Don't just meet expectations...challenge all assumptions!

Make sure clients don't feel "trapped" in a situation…the remedy is choice. But make sure you have a recommendation with rationale!

The shortening of time increases the importance of keeping an eye on the long term implication of every fast paced decision.

♥ **Need category experience? People, not agencies, have the sector experience. #newbusiness**

The future of media will constantly change but as humans we have one constant question: How will this product help/enhance me?

E-auction for a new client? Think carefully. This is not the mindset for a long-term relationship that values talent and partnership.

Genuine passion is contagious. Don't try to fake it!

Failure is success inside out. Learn from big and small failures. Most importantly, share the valuable insights you've learned with clients!

♥ **It's difficult to design products by focus groups. People often don't know what they want until you show it to them. Bloomberg Businessweek**

Presenting a new concept? Psychology studies show that people trust an idea more after it has been repeated a minimum of 3 times.

Highlight the talent of the team member. Don't ask each member to do everything equally well. Push the limits of the individuals' specialty.

newbiz@agencyname.com as the contact email address on your website...REALLY?! You may as well just say no one is dedicated to new business!

Great accomplishments are possible only through great relationships!

Generalists and specialists must become interdependent. Passion is powerful. Everything else is the price of entry.

♥ **Intelligence is more important than creative wow. And research is the wow factor that grabs attention.**

New business is serious business but remember to smile. People who smile more are often considered more competent!

Research and intelligence is the foundation of creative WOW factor...

Agencies must have their own identity, personality and culture... that matches the prospective marketer.

Small agency? Generate more appeal by creating a narrow niche... hyper-focus on a specific target, category or discipline.

Creativity is vital but driving culture through content is king!

Look for the shared values...as resonance increases, resistance decreases.

♥ **Only when you're completely honest with yourself can you be of invaluable service to others. #newbusiness**

"1 great person = 3 good people. Pay 50-100% above avg. Good for the employee, clients AND company. 3x productivity for 2x labor cost.

Redesigning your agency's website? Offer interactivity and provide reasons to come back for more information.

♥ **Culture isn't a bunch of values hanging on a wall. Its beliefs brought to life daily through current and new relationships. #newbusiness**

Redesigning your agency's website? Lead with benefits and results instead of capabilities...

IBM Study: 4 change drivers that are shifting control w/in the advertising industry: attention, creativity, measurement, ad inventories.

The most valuable asset the agency owns? It's reputation.

Don't offer the obvious solution! Be insightful, innovative and predictive when evaluating the real problem!

Set up for successful and easy communications by having ONE point of contact who is completely competent for the client's needs.

♥ **When you sign up to be creative, you sign up to fail...and that's a vital part of success. #newbusiness @brenebrown #howdesignlive**

Success is failure inside out and failure is trying to please everyone. #newbusiness

The future of advertising: Evoke confidence and demonstrate an understanding of what the consumer needs on their terms.

The future of advertising: need to be nimble enough to recognize what needs to be done & structured enough to get it done... organized chaos!

The future of advertising: tell the broad story not just soundbites. WOMoconomics is the new economics for brand advocates spreading word of mouth.

Engaging agency websites: USP; Value Offer; Case Study Support; Culture; Experience/Expertise; Easy Navigation

Create competitive advantage at intersection of core strengths.

Tough times put most small businesses on the defensive. The best offense is a good defense but defense doesn't score. Think creatively.

Every agency has one unique proprietary tool...your PEOPLE! Showcase their expertise in RFIs and collateral.

Shared values and interests are a far more powerful aggregator of human beings than demographic categories.

The best resolution is not taking sides but looking at the third side instead.

♥ **Your competitors could also be your advocates at times. Be sure to build friendly and supportive relationships. #newbusiness**

When agencies are in the thick of the pitch, they do everything and anything to keep their competitors at bay but also want to find out everything they can about them. Yes, when the pitch is on you need to fight the good fight. But I recently heard about a group of agencies who competed for a QSR account who all lost the pitch. They decided to send each other consolation prizes and congratulated each other for making it to the finalists round even though none of them prevailed. It not only took some of the sting out of the loss, but also helped to build comradery and stronger relationships with each other. Hey, you never know where opportunity can come from...even from your competitor.

Look not at how many people interact with the page, but at how many discussions are led by the readers.

More marketing dollars toward social media...why? The more you contribute to the conversation, the better off you'll be!

Ideas become more powerful when they belong to more than one person. How do you test a good idea? See how many people want to claim it!

Social media & content marketing go hand-in-hand...useful content that adds value to the online conversation and to people's lives is vital!

♥ **FAILURE: first attempt in learning, understanding, realizing, executing.**

Given the increase in media usage, media must become not only complimentary to planning and creative development but also 100% integrated!

"Real" conversations = real engagement = real results

Execution is crucial but don't forget to consistently advise, educate and inform.

♥ **Losing is a powerful motivator as long as you learn from the experience. #newbusiness**

Connect to individuals' feelings...why people act in a certain way is more important than whom or how.

Is the traditional agency model inefficient? Avoid duplication, digitize process & streamline local costs without losing the creative idea!

Agencies must make contributions in strategic marketing in order to enhance new business opportunities, revenue and profit.

The greatest possession you (or your agency) have is your reputation! Be true. Be sincere. Be a partner in the trenches!

3 "musts" for great social-media communicators: great storytellers; technical expertise w/social media; comfort with the unknown.

Digital is not traditional messages imported to the web; it can expand a product's value & build relationships in ways traditional cannot.

❤ **What teams improvise well? Teams that like each other. Build rapport and build new biz! #newbusiness**

The message isn't communicated unless it is received AND accepted! The acceptance is the beginning of advocacy.

Virgin & JetBlue changed consumer opinion by changing the way we think about the industry...not by a "new name" on the same 'ole category.

Brands with high NPS? Apple, Trader Joe's, Amazon, Zappos. Why? They're engaging, relevant, real and offer solutions for daily events.

We are a "non-commitment culture." Offer free trials or "samples" of your services to exemplify value and build brand loyalty!

❤ **Stop worrying about being "different." Instead, strive to be distinct!**

The sales funnel has shifted to a consumer voyage. AIDA now includes research and social sharing!

90% of shoppers research online prior to buying; 50+% rely on reviews before making decisions. Facebk/Twitter are trusted sources.

Instead of trying to funnel the universe down to a handful, we should focus on the handful and figure out how to make them "advangelists."

Define your higher mission beyond the bottom line...let it keep your company alive and allow it to thrive.

Protect and nurture your brand name. It's the most sustainable competitive advantage known to business.

♥ **If you end up failing. Fail fast and more importantly, fail forward!**

Can you charge a premium for the same product that can be purchased elsewhere? No...then you don't have a valuable brand name.

♥ **Don't fear failure. Let failure fuel you!**

Can your competitors offer a comparable alternative? Become the extraordinary example where consumers can't find an acceptable replacement.

If your company went out of business, would anyone miss you? Create a strong emotional connection to the brand..."loyalty beyond rationale."

We're going from a credit to debit culture with a permanent move to conservative spending.

Many studies show that multitasking slows productivity but answering the phone or an email while doing another task can be important.

Every agency needs a "new business center." Dedicate a room w/in your office that is organized focused on nothing but new business.

Develop a new biz process where a mngr is held accountable for the efforts. When everyone is in charge of new biz, no one is responsible!

Don't derail your new biz pipeline! The best time to step up the effort is when you're busiest but always set realistic goals.

SlideShare works well w/PowerPoint/Keynote while extending the life of your presentation and reach online.

Trusted content trumps viral content. Be educational and share useful info...the trust will quickly build.

**♥ Don't be a "one size fits all" agency. Be an expert & a trustworthy source. Define who you are or someone else will do it (wrong) for you.**

Service trumps sensational! Build brand advocates and point out the results from your efforts.

Carefully consider the smallest details...it's the biggest difference between you and your competitors.

Micromanaging? It's counterproductive. Let team members take responsibility for their own action...it won't happen if you micromanage.

Targeting Mom? Moms like stories. Social media is about communicating—telling a story—NOT selling.

♥ **There are leaders and those who lead. Leaders hold onto authority. Those who lead inspire. Be sure to inspire your prospects and clients.**

Is there an emotional need that is the driving force behind your brand or service? Then TV is still a GREAT way to connect w/ customers.

The agency of the future: generating creative ideas that aren't traditional ads...

The Miracle of the Result is in the Discipline, not the Talent: discipline is what separates human accomplishment from human failure.

Do you have a culturally competent environment? Assess and challenge biases in order to change behavior.

Implement "inclusive behaviors" - give/seek feedback, accept responsibility, value individual differences, make mutual contacts.

Are you succeeding as an individual but failing as a group? Be sure to cultivate and encourage diversity!

❤ **How do you determine great creative work? You feel it in your gut. #newbusiness**

Individuality is the new religion not being like the Joneses! Owning or experiencing something no one else has is the ultimate status fix.

Next trend of online experience? Relevant...to that specific moment!

When the problem is solved the solution is usually simple!

❤ **Only when you're completely honest with yourself can you be of invaluable service to others. #newbusiness**

Light on the marketing budget? Excellent service leads to word-of-mouth referrals and superior client service is no accident.

Servicing is the new selling whether it's for brands helping consumers or agencies helping marketers.

The new advertising agency model? "Tradigital" - through the line, fully integrated, "share-worthy" thinking that builds brand communities!

Have a "Proprietary" process? So does everyone else. Bottom line...it is not as unique as you think it is. Turn the process into diagnostics.

HootSuite helps you to understand perceptions misconceptions about your product/service & give you a chance to respond conversationally.

Advertising that's informative/newsworthy often performs better than trad. brand advg. Why? Because we like what's new & tire of the old.

The best media space you can buy is in someone's mind!

♥ **Be obsessed by the outcome created, not the output made.**

Global consumption of social media increased 82% w/in 1 yr. Great brand bldg tool but for ROI, use them to share info get to know your aud.

Education will be the top driver of eco growth in the developing world for the next 10yrs improving educ in women is especially effective!

Innovative ideas? Richest source of insight, ideas, data, info = employees. Their work interactions w/the product make biz what it is.

♥ **Making meetings engaging and inspiring is the first rule of any successful business! #newbusiness**

Q: unique capabilities that give you a competitive advantage in the mktplce? A: exemplify YOUR value how you measure against your compet.

Q: top industry trends how do you react to trends? A: show you're abreast of trends & they're leveraged to give clients compet advantage.

How do you provide better thought leadership than competitors? Show leadership; strategic thinking, innovative media; analytics value prop

Happy team members make for happy customers. Period. End. There is a praise deficit in almost all companies. Express gratitude for great work and accomplishments!

Ask team members in your company, "What matters the most to you right now?" and try to help them accomplish that goal.

♥ **Agency teams with a "growth mind-set" see challenges as opportunities to broaden skills and the brand. #newbusiness**

Ad Agency of the Future: greater knowledge of digital space, more "pull" interactions, leverage virtual communities.

64% of customers prefer highly personalized communication vs generic offers. Higher preference = higher response rates!

The value of your services is defined by the client's perception of the person managing the sale.

Are there lessons learned in e-mail marketing that we can apply to social media? 5. Take chances and learn from your mistakes.

Are there lessons learned in e-mail marketing that we can apply to social media? 4.Be prepared to justify your investment.

Are there lessons learned in e-mail marketing that we can apply to social media? 3.Know your best customers treat them special.

Are there lessons learned in e-mail marketing that we can apply to social media? 2. Create many opportunities to share.

Are there lessons learned in e-mail marketing that we can apply to social media? 1. Provide your customers with relevant content.

"General mkt" is now "cultural hybridity"(consmrs define themselves in many ways) via "cultural bumping"(choosing from influential factors).

♥ **Your actions are critical, and mood and actions together must resonate with your org and with reality to increase success. #newbusiness**

True values extend beyond the bounds of brand books. They are anchored in human emotions, concerns, aspirations and ambitions.

Character is what makes you who you are and helps you accomplish what you want.

♥ **Redesigning your website? Add a downloadable single sheet fact sheet to the site!**

Creativity must be an essential part of corporate culture. It needs to be ingrained in the institutions that define employees' daily lives.

In the spirit of Christmas, practice global diplomacy. Engage friends AND foes in dialogue and listen to their POVs. Merry Christmas! Encourage employees to ask themselves, "What can I do to increase my experience of happiness meaning at work?"

What is a brand? A shared GUT FEELING by the masses because we're all EMOTIONAL beings…

Relevance drives response relationships. Use the power of precision marketing to better engage customers.

Irrelevance = disengagement!

Developing direct mail? Connect with consumers encourage them to behave/respond first. The actual message is secondary often passive!

Need to re-engage top talent? Human connection drives morale. Stay connected to employees and have an open door policy…with everything.

Looking for the truth? It can be found only when reason is coupled with faith.

Need to trawl Twittersphere and the blogosphere fast? Twittorati can help you skim for leads fast.

Can't say sorry? Apologies = sign of strength. Adversity = opportunity to show true colors. A remarkable leader is able to simply apologize.

❤ **Not much good can come from a relationship where the client thinks ideas from 2 different agencies are interchangeable.**

Doing well despite downturn: Dunkin' Donuts-taps all media and messaging to gain new consumers and keeps current consumers engaged.

Trust drives profit. It's what consumers want & share... everywhere! It's the most valuable corporate asset.

Customer service: key differentiator for companies that offer similar products/services.

It's been said before but worth repeating: Customer acquisition is an investment, but profitability is built on customer retention.

What makes an outstanding leader? Not IQ or technical skills but instead, emotional intelligence.

Who's got the monkey? Support your direct reports' growth; empower them to solve their own problems, allowing you to focus on your real job

♥ **Culture is part of a promise that agencies make to its clients. Be sure it's clear and contagious. #newbusiness**

Questions to ask the mngr in the mirror: Am I communicating a vision priorities? Bldg in scheduled think time? Cultivating relationships?

Want to know how your employees REALLY feel? Don't rely on reports. Walk the halls & be approachable! Talk to them...but LISTEN more.

Doing well despite downturn: Walmart-value proposition helped customers come to trust the company that will help "Save Money. Live Better."

♥ **No mistakes in improv unless someone recognizes it. It's a team sport & everyone supports each other. Apply it to new biz! #newbusiness**

Remember the oft-used acronym TEAM...Together Everyone Accomplishes More!

3 Rs of recession mktg: Retention, Repurchase, Referral. Bottom line - focus on customer loyalty now more than ever!

The biggest impact businesses suffer during a down turn? The shift in sales peoples' attitudes - they accept all excuses from prospects.

Found a scathingly negative review of your product online? Don't post a fake positive review. LISTEN to the constructive criticism!

Selling software? It's not the technology consumers are buying... it's the service and the team! Empower your employees!

Key to corporate success: Dynamism + Trust. And trust is becoming more important than dynamism.

A true leader always expresses appreciation knows people are motivated for THEIR OWN reasons not YOURS!

Microsoft believes we're in the era of willingness! Everyone is willing to work together, be efficient and make things happen as a team!

Are you fortunate enough to hire? Behavioral assessments will help to build an "engaged workforce" who want to feel ownership in a company.

Level of employee ownership in a company=high levels of customer satisfaction loyalty. "The Ownership Quotient"-sense of ownership matters.

Don't tell people to innovate...not the goal. Create a culture that allows for ideas, improvements and potential to change for the better.

❤ **What blocks collaboration? Fear. Don't be afraid to fail since failure is success inside out. #newbusiness**

Harness the power of others by leading, not micro-managing! It requires character, competence, connection.

C. Anderson's, Free The Future of a Radical Price...free is a biz strategy that is essential for survival. Freemium is the new Premium!

Offer outstanding service to employees, vendors, clients; Outstanding Service=Speechless Smiles!

Be nimble, innovative, service-oriented. To get ahead in the downturn you must disrupt industries, trends markets. Show the value-added!

Be upbeat connect with high-energy people who share similar business issues. It costs nothing to smile... And it makes a difference!

Really listen to customers, employees, vendors, colleagues take action comments. Report back to those who shared ideas on changes made.

Value dignity in every business decision invariably it will make your company more competitive. Need proof? One word...Zappos!

Leading isn't about vision or pathfinding, writes Joe Grenny, it's about being able to intentionally influence behavior in a desirable way.

Who emerges in a recession? Unique traits? Common characteristic: passion for innovation. 3 drivers: guts, mgmt, willingness to act.

♥ **14% trust ads; 18% trust bloggers; 92% trust word of mouth from friends. Create brand advocates!**

The "new frugality" isn't fleeting! Consumer psychology has changed and that mindset will remain when the downturn ends.

Good managers help employees succeed in whatever role they happen to be in. Great managers see unique talents of each employee and create roles!

We all "want" ROI but we forget to "do" ROI...build Relationships, impact Outcomes and make Improvements!

Doing well despite downturn: Charles Schwab-restored people's confidence in investing focused on gaining trust...proved all was not lost.

@ The Power of Small book interview...it's the smallest actions that make the most profound impact in life!

@ The Power of Small book interview...story re: P&G CEO. A.G. Lafley NEVER uses the word "I" in any speech he gives. WE & OUR drives success!

Pressure to deliver accountability? Investing behind mktg efforts that deliver calculated ROI is a model for a stable market.

♥ **Your agency's greatest weakness or greatest strength? It's people. Be sure to invest in them.**

The desire to win is a key driver to success but desire alone doesn't win. Creativity and structure are both necessary to improve the odds!

Relationships without sales is a social friendship. Sales without a relationship is just a mere transaction!

♥ **Are your employees treating your clients the same way you are treating your employees? Empower employees and allow them to be exceptional!**

Patience, comm skills effective time mgmt don't show up on a resume but are invaluable assets that determine successful biz relationships!

Put the "custom" back in customer! Customer service may be the best differentiator against your competition.

High profile marketers must have these qualities: comfort in limelight, being held accountable, most importantly, tolerate pressure!

Recession = increase use of social media. Why? As trust in companies deteriorate, the friendship model increases. Advocacy = Value

♥ **Why? You must be clear on "the why" – it is the purpose behind everything you do. It's vital for bringing clarity and focus to the end goal.**

Good business is all about serving at a profit NOT selling at a profit!

Command control communication short-circuits the spirit of consumer experience engagement which is about opportunity, not obligation.

Seek out practical savvy instinct when making business decisions. Wisdom is the experience of a lifetime and is often the best advice!

*The Fred Factor*: 1st principle reminds me of a NYC cab driver who wears a chauffeur's suit and treats you like you're in a limo.

The swarm is about actively sharing intelligence. You can't lead a swarm. The real new media today is people!

Influence is one of the most valuable assets a brand can have... they command attention.

♥ **Visual content is the key to driving emotional connections - it's a free pass to the emotional side of your brain. #ANAMasters #newbusiness**

The notion of a swarm is not to appeal to everyone. Conviction, collaboration and creativity influence swarms.

The future of Mktg is to influence communities not individuals.

Still need to market to the herd but swarms have become vital. You may not like change but becoming irrelevant is worse!

The #1 value proposition that is vital in a recession is to guarantee SHORT-term benefits. One year ROI or less.

Innovation and directness is vital during this transformation. Change or die.

Flat is the new black right now! The recession will end but the face of business has changed forever. Core values are now at the center.

Forrester top 5 consumer trends presentation: Superior customer experience will differentiate top firms-not price and product!

Join the conversation through various channels by becoming a "tradigital" ad agency!

♥ **Live with your prospects' problems. Laugh with your current clients. Love what you do!**

Once again, the client team was deadlocked between two agencies. This time it was for a regional QSR brand and they debated for hours in the hotel conference room over which agency to select. The agencies were comparable in every which way. It came down to one question posed by the CEO, "At the end of the day, which agency would you rather have a beer with at the bar?" Cliché? Yes. But so true. Of course, there's lots of data, research, strategic thinking and all the science that goes into winning a pitch. Is it vital? You bet. However, we are also in the business of relationships. It's apparent when agencies love what they do and enjoy each other as a team. And it's often contagious. Keep the chemistry alive throughout the pitch and after the win. Don't become complacent, live in your client's shoes, love what you do and have fun...it's those relationships that stay healthy and vibrant that endure long past the pitch and for many more years beyond the industry average.

# PART VI: ADVICE FROM THE LEGENDS

Education increases knowledge but life breeds wisdom. There are many great teachers in the world. Some we remember from our childhood. Others are media celebrities. And a few have made an impact that changed humankind as a result of their vision. I've learned from the successes and failures of others over the years. I've benefited from their stories. I've grown from their shared wisdom. These quotes are a compilation from legends past and present that I've admired in one way or another. These words of wisdom have helped me to be a better search consultant for agencies and clients. They've helped me to build a new business tool called Access Confidential, and a strong team who truly cares about agencies' new business success. These words have also made me a better business partner, business owner and friend to others in the industry along the way. I know you will see the relevance between their thoughts and this crazy (but cool) world of communications.

♥ **"Difference b/t successful people & very successful people? VS people say no to almost everything. They're selective!" W. Buffett #newbusiness**

"Good relationships don't just happen. They take time, patience and people who truly want to be together." Author Unknown. #newbusiness

As ideas evolve, don't lose sight of the goal. "There needs to be someone who is the keeper & 'reiterator' of the vision," Jobs. #newbusiness

"Reset expectations. Don't raise them since raised expectations tend to be exponential & can lead to disappointment." Seth Godin #newbusiness

"Chase the vision, not the money, the money will end up following you." - Tony Hsieh #newbusiness

♥ **"IQ makes you smart but CQ (cultural quotient) makes you relevant," M.Young, WW Chair & CEO, Ogilvy & Mather. #forbescmosummit #newbusiness**

"Social metrics are nice but business metrics are better," Carolyn Everson of Facebook. #newbusiness

"ROI = Return On Ignoring" J. Hayzlett #ANAMasters #newbusiness

♥ **"I want the agency to feel the soul of my brand!" Quoted from a marketer searching for an agency. #newbusiness**

"It doesn't take an ounce of talent to play hard!" Derek Jeter. #newbusiness

"Older people create pop culture by looking at the young. The young doesn't create pop culture." Ben, CEO, Cheezburger Network. #thenewpop

"Consumption of media has changed but people are still the same." Perez Hilton #thenewpop

"The secret of success is sincerity. Once you can fake that, you've got it made." George Burns

❤ **"It would be difficult being blind if I didn't have any vision." H.Keller. Think about how appropriate that attitude is for new biz success.**

"Our companies need innovation, and they need a customer focus." Stephen Quinn, former CMO, Walmart

"The artist hasn't discovered possibilities in new media & digital & how to use tech to beautifully & intelligently express brands." L. Clow

❤ **"If you want ACTION, don't write. Go and tell the guy what you want." David Ogilvy**

"Mobile advertising is the future of consumer experience," Barry Judge, former CMO, Best Buy

"Most people use research in the same way a drunk uses a lamp post: for support rather than illumination." David Ogilvy

♥ **"Minimalism is not a lack of something. It's simply the perfect amount of something." Nicholas Burroughs. In other words: KISS! #newbusiness**

"Treat your brand like a political campaign," says Ron Faris. Help marketers figure out the message & then develop propaganda around it!

"Everyone is inherently creative but true creativity is inhibited partly since it's educated out of us! See beyond the obvious." Rick Boyko

♥ **"It's not what you say, it's what people hear." Frank Luntz. #newbusiness**

Stewarding the account? Go beyond expectation. No one ever got fired for over servicing. "It's never crowded along the extra mile," W.Dyer.

"5 characteristics of great leaders that endure: brave, caring, disciplined, smart and trustworthy." Sun Tzu.

"Implication rather than explication is a powerful lesson we can take away from stories (& apply to brand bldng)." Jim Signorelli

"...have to deliver his message in a different way - memorably & artfully - if he was going to be "chosen" by the consumer." Bernbach

♥ **"There's 1 boss: The customer. He can fire everybody in the company, from the top down, simply by spending his money somewhere else." Disney**

"Work w/o conviction, effectiveness, personality is cold arithmetic instead of warm persuasion." Bernbach

"We can do no great things-only small things w/love," Mother Teresa. Do what you love, love what you do, give your all to everything you do.

♥ **"You can listen to what people say, sure. But you will be far more effective if you listen to what people do." Seth Godin**

"Whatever you vividly imagine, ardently desire, sincerely believe enthusiastically act upon...must inevitably come to pass." Paul J. Meyer

"Patience is the key element in success." Bill Gates

"In life business, there are two cardinal sins. The 1st is to act precipitously without thought the 2nd is to not act at all." Carl Icahn

♥ **Definition of a genius: "The man who can do the average thing when all those around him are going crazy." Napoleon #newbusiness**

"Work bears a particular mark of man of humanity, the mark of a person operating within a community of persons." PJPII

"A little Consideration, a little Thought for Others, makes all the difference." Winne the Pooh

"The service we render others is the rent we pay for our room on earth." Wilfred Grenfell

❤ **"Relevance is the new unaided brand awareness metric," Matt Jauchius, EVP & CMO, Nationwide. #forbescmosummit #newbusiness**

"There's been a shift in focus on values not just economics to consumers....looking more closely at who is selling them what." D. Mitchell

"People want to do what they think others will do," Cialdini. It's the most powerful motivator for influencing change!

❤ **Personalized mktg at scale is the biggest trend that Facebook is seeing according to C. Everson, VP Global Mktg Solutions. #ForbesCMOSummit**

 "The dictionary is the only place where success comes before work!" Vince Lombardi

"Stay close to your customers. Implement decisions quickly retain the flexibility to adapt. Take some risks. And enjoy the ride." S. Godin

"Success isn't about being perceived as the best at what you do, it's about being perceived as the ONLY one who does what you do!" J. Garcia

"Judge a man by his questions rather than his answers," Voltaire. Especially true in sales process. Ask the right questions solve problems

♥ **"I do not think about consumers. I think about people."
Craig Dubitsky, Founder of hello products #ANAMasters
#newbusiness**

The best advice from Warren Buffet: "Keep it simple. Boil things down, work on the things that really count, think through the basics."

"Empower subordinates. Solicit opinions before giving yours allow people to feel confident in their plan." L. Blankfein, CEO, Goldman Sachs

"Show, don't tell. A good manager must be a good teacher. A lot of very bright people lose sight of that." Jim Sinegal, Co-Founder, Costco

♥ **"Understand the top line business and send a custom package. I delete all unsolicited emails." NASCAR marketer.
#newbusiness**

The Best Advice I Ever Got: "Fanaticism is underrated." Bill Gates.

3 critical sales factors: talk to the right people, build relationships use changes in buyers environment. Good thoughts from N. Edelshain

"Many a small thing has been made large by the right kind of advertising." Mark Twain

70% of executives say "staying abreast of technology" is a top anxiety. "We are drowning in information but starved for knowledge." Naisbitt

♥ **"Tell me what you're great at and don't sell me everything!" Brian Harrington, ZipCar. #newbusiness**

"Added Value = total value MINUS the value without you," B. Nalebuff. Great guideline when prospecting new clients evaluating current ones.

You can't do good business without having a high IQ... Implementation Quotient! "Execution is the chariot of genius." William Blake

"A recession presents opportunities that aren't available in a bullish mkt...be insightful." W. Buffet

"Mktg tip through a crisis: FOCUS! Do few things really well as opposed to trying to continue biz as usual." Nick Utton, CMO E-Trade

♥ **"All agencies start out different but end up the same." Frank Lowe. Be sure to have a distinctive POV and live it! #newbusiness**

"A brand for a company is like a reputation for a person. You earn reputation by trying to do hard things well." Jeff Bezos

"The key to a leader's impact is sincerity. Before he can inspire, he must be swayed himself. To convince, he must himself believe." Churchill

A fact wrapped in a story is 22x more memorable than the mere pronouncement of that fact, according to cognitive psychologist Jerome Bruner.

"We should take care not to make the intellect our GOD; it has, of course, powerful muscles but no personality." Einstein

J. Wren, M. Roth, & Sir Martin Sorrell new biz recommendation: Reflect your market in the diversity of your team & focus on your people.

John Wren, Michael Roth, & Sir Martin Sorrell new biz recommendation: Use data and analytics to generate consumer insights.

John Wren, Michael Roth, & Sir Martin Sorrell new biz recommendation: Keep pace with new technology and new media.

♥ **"Big data does nothing without the big ideas!" CMO Mary Kay #newbusiness**

Disney boss: Corporate life demands patience and optimism.

♥ **"Live a good life. In the end it's not the yrs in a life but a life in the yrs," Lincoln. Put "life" in clients' biz & have many yrs w/them!**

## PART VII: AS SEEN IN THE PRESS

I'm always flattered, delighted and sometimes even surprised by the outpouring of kind remarks I receive after I write an article that's published or after speaking at a conference. I often think, "I'm just sharing my knowledge to help others succeed."

I've greatly enjoyed writing and speaking, as well as managing reviews for clients searching for new agencies, over the past 15 years. I get a sense of fulfillment from teaching and joy from seeing how I've made a small contribution toward helping others become more successful.

The following section is a compilation of all the new business articles I've written that have been published throughout my career. I hope they're a reminder of some vital lessons to keep in mind when prospecting, pitching and stewarding accounts.

ARTICLES PUBLISHED:

- **How Culture Impacts Enduring and Mutually Beneficial Relationships**
  The Huffington Post, November 23, 2015

- **Want to Win Your Next New Business Pitch? Channel the Characteristics of a Champion.**
  HubSpot's Agency Post, September 17, 2015
  The Huffington Post, September 14, 2015

- **The Sins and Saviors of Business Meetings**
  The Huffington Post, July 26, 2015

- **New Business Success? It's About Caring, Not Selling**
  Forbes, July 22, 2015

- **No Laughing Matter…How Improv Improves Business.**
  The Huffington Post, May 18, 2015

- **A Man's Best Friend Can Teach A Few Things About A Man's Best Business Practices**
  LinkedIn, March 26, 2015

- **Can Improv Improve Marketing?**
  Forbes, December 1, 2014

- **Why Clients Should Cut Ties with Incumbent Agencies Sooner**
  Forbes, September 22, 2014

- **Prospecting Needs to Be Treated Like NFL Footballs**
  HubSpot's Agency Post, March 3, 2014

- **CMOs Shifting Brands from Nouns to Verbs**
  Forbes, November 6, 2013

- **Human Experience: The New Media Channel**
  Forbes, July 3, 2013

- **Starting a new agency? Thoughts you should consider before turning the key in the door**
  Fuelingnewbusiness.com, July 9, 2013

- **Calling an Agency Review? Top Three Reasons Why the CMO should be Part of the Process from the Start!**
  Forbes, September 19, 2012

- **Uniting the Masses Will Help Single You Out**
  UprisingMovements.com, January 25, 2012

- **Treat Your Clients Like Prospects and Vice Versa**
  Advertising Age, August 13, 2010

- **Cracking the Clutter! What Babies Can Teach Ad Agency New Business Executives about Prospecting**
  4A's Business Development Blog, October 30, 2009

- **A Perfect Storm Warrants a Perfect Plan**
  Adweek, August 31, 2008

- **First, Do No Harm. What Doctors Can Teach Agencies about Relationships.**
  Adweek, April 28, 2008

- **Chemistry is More than Just an Attraction**
  TalentZoo.com, January 2008

## How Culture Impacts Enduring and Mutually Beneficial Relationships

By: Lisa Colantuono

As an agency search consultant, I often get asked, "What wins the pitch?" The simple answer is: chemistry. Strong chemistry between client and agency teams is vital. But chemistry goes much deeper than just wanting to have a beer with someone. It's really all about culture.

Even after fourteen years of running agency reviews, I find one of the most critical meetings between prospective clients and agencies is that first initial face-to-face meeting that hopefully takes place at the agency. While this meeting is typically referred to as the Chemistry Meeting, perhaps a more apt name would be the Cultural Affinity Meeting. This is the first opportunity the client has to meet your team - but more importantly it allows them to get a true sense of your agency's culture before they go through the arduous process of evaluating and selecting an agency partner. In fact, one of the key objectives of the Chemistry Meeting is to "weed out" those agencies that simply aren't the right fit.

I recently sat down with Andrew Graff, CEO of Advertising Agency Allen & Gerritsen (A&G), to get his perspective on how an agency's culture - its "reason for being" - can be articulated during the pitch process. A&G has a truly unique culture and they've been recognized for that culture by being named Advertising's "Best Place to Work" by Advertising Age two years running. For shops like A&G, building a culture where you

165

can be inspired to come to work every day is one thing, but translating that culture to clients during a quick courtship is often challenging. He offers the following tried and true tips:

## Be True To Who You Are

Every agency search begins and ends with culture. You must seek out partnerships that not only allow you to remain true to whom you are, but those that complement your differences. Having a distinct culture has worked well for agencies like Concept Farm with its farm-like theme to help cultivate ideas, The Richards Group with its infamous stairwell to build camaraderie and communication, and The Barbarian Group with its one long desk that meanders through the office, where everyone shares a seat at the same table. Culture is part of a promise that agencies make to their clients and having a distinctive culture is the best way to demonstrate real differentiation from the vast sea of agencies out there.

## Bring Your A-Game - And Your A-Team

When participating in an agency review, agencies need to put together the best team based on relevant experience, talent and passion about the brand. Perhaps even more important is to have people at the table that can best articulate, demonstrate and make relevant to the prospective client, their unique agency culture. The question going through every client's mind: "Why do they want to work on my brand?" There's a difference between wanting to work on an airline account and wanting to work on American Airlines. Why? Because American has a distinct culture, a unique set of values and a specific mission, which differ from other airlines. Clearly, having an agency team of tightly-knit co-workers who genuinely like and respect each other, is the price of entry.

But clients are yearning for more than just camaraderie. They want an agency that truly understands their unique culture and can demonstrate how their own culture will have a positive and significant impact on their business.

## Wear Your Passion On Your Sleeve

Demonstrate to clients that you want to work on their brand - not just in their category - and do it from the very first connection you make with them. Whether it's during prospecting or within the course of a review, make it crystal clear what attracted your agency to that particular brand. Compare and contrast their brand to others in the category. Talk about positive interactions/experiences your team members have had with the brand. Explain how and why your agency's culture complements the prospective client's culture. Show them the attention and affection you will demonstrate should you be lucky enough to win their business - all because it's simply part of the agency culture to do so.

## New Business Is A Two Way Street

Use the review process to vet the client's culture as much as they are vetting yours. This is a critical piece of the review process that too many agencies miss. They get so dazzled by the potential revenue and/or prestige the client brand will bring to the agency that they forget to make certain that the client is actually a good match for the agency's culture. Do they demonstrate the same level of risk-taking on which your agency thrives? Are they open to new ideas and new approaches? Will they let you do the kind of work that has made you - and your existing clients - successful? The answers to these questions are not always easy to ascertain - but the best agencies find ways to assess whether or not the potential exists to work with each prospective client in a way that will be mutually beneficial to both client and agency. And when that doesn't appear to be the case, bow out. It will be the best thing you can do for your agency - and for the client.

These tips are essential to help prevail in the new business process. Cultural alignment is so critical to the success and endurance of client/agency relationships, the ANA (Association of National Advertisers) and the 4As (American Association of Advertising Agencies) have issued agency search guidelines to help brands to properly evaluate prospective agency partners from the very start.

As an agency, you too should develop your specific guidelines and requirements to help assess cultural compatibility. In the long run these guidelines will be one of your most important new business tools, allowing you to establish and maintain the best client relationships and garner the respect of everyone in your agency.

Lisa Colantuono is Co-President of AAR Partners, an agency search consultancy since 1980, helping marketers to find the best communications agencies for their marketing needs.

**Place of first publication: Huffington Post, November 23, 2015**

# Want to Win Your Next Pitch? Channel the Characteristics of a Champion

By: Lisa Colantuono

Tickets for the US Open's women's final this past weekend hit a high of $1,500 on StubHub before Serena Williams' devastating loss to the unseeded Italian, Roberta Vinci, after which prices dropped to as little as $62 after her win. Thousands of tennis and even non-tennis fans were cheering on Serena as she would have been the first woman to match Steffi Graf's Grand Slam (victory in all four major tournaments in a calendar-year sweep) in 1988.

Only three women have achieved that feat: Maureen Connolly in 1953, Margaret Court in 1970, and Graf -- the swift and serious German aptly nicknamed "Fraulein Forehand" by the American tennis writer Bud Collins.

"I think she lost her way, mentally," said Serena's coach, Patrick Mouratoglou, in an interview with USA Today. "Tactically, she didn't know what to do at a certain point. When you make the wrong choices, you lose the points that you're used to winning, and then you don't understand what's happening, and then you make more and more wrong choices."

But let's give credit where credit is due and highlight the fact that this champion holds a 2015 major streak at 26 straight matches.

But what makes a champion? And what can we learn from this that applies to new business pitching?

Champions share many characteristics, none of which are determined by their talents. Here are some of those characteristics that pave the path to success to keep in mind.

**A champion has the courage to risk failure, knowing that setbacks are lessons from which to learn.**

In terms of new business, marketers want innovative thinking, and agencies need to be willing to take intelligent risks to demonstrate creative ideas that are more than just ads. They need to realize that not all clients may agree with the agency's perspective, but there may be a compromise position that will lead to ROI. The best agencies (and clients) know exactly what makes for a successful relationship.

**A champion trains her thought processes as well as her body to produce a total approach to performance.**

Similarly in pitching, marketers need a total approach to their brand issues. They crave holistic business solution, taking into account how the creative idea will work across disciplines including direct, digital, content marketing, public relations, and more.

**A champion understands that competitors provide the challenge and the motivation to improve – and win.**

However, champions stay focused on their game and not what the other person is doing when in the moment. There isn't a review that happens where at least one agency asks the question, "How many agencies received the RFI? Or who has been invited to pitch?" While there is value in knowing who your competition is and what your chances of winning are, it's better to study your primary competition *before* a pitch process. Don't waste precious pitch time focusing on your competition.

**A champion concentrates on one point at a time and doesn't get overwhelmed by thinking about winning the entire game all at once.**

There is rationale behind every step of a review process, and more importantly, there are specific goals to reach for each step. When agencies start thinking too far ahead and try to win the business in the first meeting, they lose focus and often fail to move forward. Serena's coach blamed part of her loss to being mentally fogged. Don't lose your way mentally. The No. 1 goal of the chemistry meeting is to get invited to participate as a finalist in the remainder of the review process.

After the match, Serena said pressure did not play a role in the loss: "I told you guys I don't feel pressure. I never felt pressure," she said in an interview for the US Open. "I don't know. I never felt that pressure to win here. I said that from the beginning."

She may have tried to convince herself of the "no pressure" attitude, but let's be realistic. The pressure is real, and it creeps into every competitive situation whether it's becoming a member of the elite group of Grand Slam winners or winning a multi-million dollar piece of new business. A champion trains her thought processes to think calmly and rationally, not emotionally. Still, it is one helluva head game.

For Serena, if she continues on the path she's on, there is always next year. However, when it comes to new business, there is no "next year." There *is* always the invaluable experience, learning, thinking, and insights that can be applied to your next pitch. Just don't forget to apply the characteristics of what makes a champion a real champion.

**Place of first publication: Huffington Post, September 14, 2015; Agency Post, September 17, 2015**

# The Sins and Saviors of Business Meetings

By: Lisa Colantuono

According to Time Management Facts and Figures by Dr. Donald Wetmore, on an average day, there are 17 million meetings in America and although approximately 60 percent of attendees take notes to appear as if they are listening, nine out of ten people daydream in those meetings. We've all been in them. Meetings are the most universal - and universally despised - part of business. We often leave shaking our heads wondering what was actually accomplished but we've also attended those that were well worth the time. Meetings can either be the bane of our existence or a valuable tool in achieving goals and objectives.

"Meetings matter because that's where an organization's culture perpetuates itself," says William Daniels of American Consulting & Training. "Meetings are how an organization says, 'You are a member.' So if every day we go to boring meetings full of boring people, then we can't help but think that this is a boring company. Bad meetings are a source of negative messages about our company and ourselves."

As an agency search consultant in the ad world, I've had the privilege of attending more great meetings than I care to count – and also the misfortune of being witness to those meetings that simply spiraled south.

The big question is what are those deadly sins that leave attendees shaking their heads? And how can meetings (especially meetings with prospects) become so valuable that participants are not only pleasantly surprised, but also leave feeling empowered and wanting more?

The saviors of productive business meetings are: inform, engage and inspire.

**Inform.** Since the brain only retains 5 percent of what is stated in meetings, offering no more than a few new ideas in one meeting will help increase retention on the participant's behalf. Researchers have often debated the maximum amount of items we can store in our short-term memory, and a new study puts the limit at three or possibly four. Saying very general and important things that everyone already knows can turn a meeting into a snooze fest fast. Inform your attendees by painting pictures and evoking emotions with words. Theater of the mind is a powerful and inspiring tool.

**Engage.** One of the best ways to engage involves storytelling. Stories engage because they invite listeners to co-create the imagery of the objective - allowing those with questions, conflicts and resolutions to ultimately shape - and importantly own - the end result. In addition to stories, quick, interactive team building exercises or audience involvement are also great engagement tools. For example body polls ("With a show of hands, how many people in this room have...") involves the attendees in the meeting and they become participants rather than spectators. Another way to engage is to change up the meeting location. Meetings are often held in conference rooms that, while utilitarian, offer little to make a meeting feel exciting and interesting. Consider relocating the meeting. A new, unexpected venue creates energy, lowers filters and increases attention span.

**Inspire.** Before we get to the "how," let's start with the "why." As

Simon Sinek preaches, "People don't buy what you do, they buy why you do it." However, we're trained to talk about the "what" first which often leads to minds wondering off into never-never land. So let's first dissect the word "inspire" just to see where that takes us. Inspire is rooted in the Latin word "spirare," which means "to breathe." To "inspire" is, in a sense, to "breathe into." To inspire someone is to breathe life into them. Think Apple or Nike or Zappos or Starbucks. Starbucks doesn't sell coffee - it sells moments of connection. Apple sells innovation. Zappos sells service. Nike sells *inspiration*. And they all start with "why."

Those sins of deadly business meetings? Don't be a time hog. Share your thoughts and don't monopolize the meeting. Don't step over or talk on top of other people in the room and check your ego at the door. Remember K.I.S.S. Ideas that are too convoluted and complex will leave attendees cold -- and quite possibly, asleep. And finally, leave your cell phone on your desk when going to a meeting. Go tech-less and avoid the temptation to check emails and text messages. Instead inform, inspire and be respectful of everyone's time by showing that you're truly engaged.

If all else fails, according to research carried out by Holiday Inn, over 80 percent of business people say that the snack selection at a meeting could influence the outcome.

Lisa Colantuono is Co-President of AAR Partners, a prominent agency search consultancy since 1980 and Co-Founder of Access Confidential, a comprehensive new business prospecting tool since 2005.

**Place of first publication: Huffington Post, July 26, 2015**

## New Business Success? It's About Caring, Not Selling

This article is by Lisa Colantuono, Co-President of AAR Partners.

The backbone of professional business is the ongoing acquisition of new clients, customers or accounts. Many organizations promote the idea that "everyone is responsible" for prospecting, cultivating and signing up new accounts. The problem is that when "everyone is responsible" for new business *no one* is responsible. For those of you who subscribe to the idea that "everyone is responsible" – how's that going for you? Likely, not well.

So who are those "hot agencies" and what are they doing to consistently win new business? Bottom line, the "who" doesn't really matter. Of course, we can point to R/GA, which has won agency of the year multiple times from multiple trade associations, or The Concept Farm, which has consistently won reviews over the years; however, in each case, the DNA – the culture – of those agencies is unique and simply can't be replicated.

But there are some transferrable lessons in what they are doing to consistently win new business. What is it that puts them on a winning streak while others are relegated to the runner-up position? I've led hundreds of agency reviews over the last 14 years, and I can honestly say that it's not the individual people that make the difference. It's the team that makes the greatest impact on prospective clients.

AAR Partners recently managed a review for a hospitality account, and the CMO clearly stated three specific evaluation points he and his team kept in mind while going through the arduous deliberation process of selecting a winning agency:

1. Did the agency team build our confidence?
2. Did the agency team leave us wanting more?
3. Can we imagine working with the agency team two to three years out and see a positive ROI and a successful relationship?

Sure, clients want to work with people they like and trust but, first and foremost, they want to work with a team that works well together internally. We're in the business of relationships, and if the client team cannot project themselves working well with the agency team for the long term, the agency will most likely fall to the runner-up spot.

Yes – as it's been said, every agency's greatest asset is its people, but it's the team plus the culture that envelopes and supports that team that makes all the difference. It's the team *and* the culture that ensure consistency, even if an individual team member leaves.

So what is that cultural distinction? It's a powerful element that shapes an agency's environment, work ethic, relationships and ultimately new business success. It's that infamous stairwell at the Richards Group; it's the wall of caricatures at the Moroch that highlights employee longevity and commitment; it's the one long desk at the Barbarian Group that exemplifies camaraderie and cross-discipline thinking.

It is the team that demonstrates that culture to each and every prospective client in the following ways:

1. **Drive, determination and RFB.** The drive and determination come from within. And it's the reason for being that brings clarity and meaning. I constantly ask the agencies I meet with, "What is your reason for being?" You'd be surprised how few agencies can succinctly articulate what they do and why they are different. According to the U.S. Census data, there are more than 76,000 communications firms in the United States. So what's the reason behind another new agency to exist? The agencies that truly stand out know exactly what they stand for and why they do what they do. Take for example, Oberland, in New York. They are focused on creating, nurturing and growing brands with a higher purpose. That reason for being has fueled the agency's drive and new business growth since they were founded only a few years ago.

2. **Passion and chemistry.** Nothing beats it. And more important, you can't fake it or define it. If an explanation is necessary then the agency simply doesn't have it.

3. **Powerful and consistent technique.** This isn't about a proprietary process or point of view. Again, there's nothing proprietary at an agency except for its people. Rigor is needed in new business and most important, an integrated communications platform that reaches out to marketers in the right manner with the right message and at the right time. The late great Mike Hughes helped build The Martin Agency into what it is today by reaching out with relevant and timely information to show he was thinking about that brand and cared enough to send a note (many times handwritten, I might add) that was sincere and not "sales-y."

Unfortunately, there is no magic bullet for winning new business. It's consistent communication, diligence, passion and a culture engrained in a team that truly cares about its prospective clients' needs. Jackie Kanas, former director of advertising and public relations manager at The Guardian Life Insurance Company of America, said it best: "Persistence is important, but foster a relationship by offering business insights and not just sales information."

**Place of first publication: Forbes, July 22, 2015**

## No Laughing Matter...How Improv Improves Business.

By: Lisa Colantuono

Robin Williams will always be remembered as the improvisational genius that was forever present in the moment, and the only thing faster than his mouth was his mind. His speed and focus allowed him to feel the audience and change direction on the fly. Although Mr. Williams made improv look like riding a bike, very few people can upstage him or would even try. But was his skill innate or learned, and what can we, as business executives, study from his ability and apply to the business world?

I sat down with Bob Kulhan, the CEO and Co-Founder of Business Improvisations (http://businessimprov.com/) to understand more about how innovative thinking and smart business skills can stem from improv insights. Trained by one of today's most famous comedians, Tina Fey, he recalled words of advice from his instructor: "Don't try to be funny or clever - just support the people around you and make them look good." Not an easy bit of advice to swallow, especially living in an individualistic society. It's not your own self-promotion that is of value. It's valuing your team members' input and helping to elevate them to the next level. In his book, *Servant Leadership*, Robert Greenleaf highlights how servant leaders are attentive to growth and development of all those around them as part of their team. And as part of the curriculum at Business Improvisations, building trust and team support is one of the top three improv lessons taught.

Finding the value in others and trusting the individual's input is what knits individuals into a team that wants to be part of something bigger than themselves. This leads to the golden rule of improv being "Yes...and." This little gem helps to build momentum, innovation and relationships instead of shutting down ideas by reacting with "no...but." According to Mr. Kulhan, yes...and is the single greatest tool to suspend judgment, focus intently and not just be in the moment but embrace it. Similar to one of Robin William's explosive riffs, embracing the moment doesn't come from editing or planning. Yes...and helps to build momentum, action and trust within the team. It leads to intent listening, hanging onto every word being said and being committed to the challenge you've accepted. All crucial skills needed to succeed in business.

Improv is not all about flying by the seat of your pants. The instructors at Business Improvisations teach improv tenets that help to establish something vital for all presenters in the boardroom: to be comfortable in your own skin and let people into your world versus running the room. They also encourage failing and believe in the power of failure since the school of hard knocks is where all great improvisational geniuses became great. After recently taking a 2-hour improv course at the Manhattan Comedy School (http://www.manhattancomedyschool.com/), I can personally attest to the fact that failure is innate in improv. But it's also a team sport; there is no single star in the group since your improv group is supporting you and you them. The same applies in the presentation room. Rehearsing your subject matter is your opportunity to test delivery methods, flunk in front of friends, integrate as a cohesive team, master the material. Eventually it looks like it's all off the cuff and that you're all finishing each other's sentences.

As Bob delicately put it,

"Improv is an art form with no boundaries, just techniques to help build better relationships since the one thing that improv relies on to work effectively is people."

As in marketing and most other industries, we are in the business of relationships, and what better way to win in the boardroom than to build better relationships?

*Lisa Colantuono is Co-President of AAR Partners, a prominent agency search consultancy since 1980.*

Follow Lisa Colantuono on Twitter: www.twitter.com/AARLisa

**Place of first publication: Huffington Post, May 18, 2015**

## A Man's Best Friend Can Teach A Few Things About A Man's Best Business Practices

By: Lisa Colantuono, Co-President, AAR Partners

Just about everyone has heard the old saying "A man's best friend is his dog," highlighting their close relations, loyalty, and companionship with humans within many societies. However it's doubtful that many people know where that adage came from. It can be found in the transcript of an 1870 trial, and it was part of one of the most memorable closing arguments ever made by an attorney.

George Vest, on behalf of his client, began his closing argument with these passionate words:

"The best friend a man has in this world may turn against him and become his enemy. His son or daughter that he has reared with loving care may prove ungrateful. Those who are nearest and dearest to us, those whom we trust with our happiness and our good name, may become traitors to their faith. The money that a man has he may lose. It flies away from him perhaps when he needs it most. A man's reputation may be sacrificed in a moment of ill-considered action. The people who are prone to fall on their knees to do us honor when success is with us, may be the first to throw the stones of malice when failure settles its cloud upon our heads. The one absolutely unselfish friend that a man can have in this selfish world, the one that never deserts him, the one that never proves ungrateful or treacherous, is his dog."

The closing argument went on to paint a picture that not a single friend except a man's dog will greet him with enthusiasm, protect his master, love him unconditionally and remain noble and loyal through all situations they endure together.

What is so profound about his closing argument? It's authentic and so incredibly simple. Both of course, can be applied to the art of new business. But what about the lessons from a man's best friend and how they can be applied to our day-to-day dog-eat-dog world (the pun was just too good to pass up) of new business?

1. **Have a great attitude:** No one wants to work with a pessimist or someone who is argumentative every step of the way. Be positive when prospecting, pitching and stewarding a client relationship. Build a friendship where you consistently contribute to a successful business partnership. Not everything will be a bowl of cherries but showing that your outlook and approach to all situations is optimistic, constructive and confident will reassure the client that he has the right partner along for the ride.

2. **Explore everything:** What do clients look for in an agency relationship? They want you to be an explorer and not just an expert for their brand. Your job is to keep an ear to the ground on the next best thing, know their consumers' purchasing journey and keep discovering new insights based on the overly abundant data available on our digital dashboards. "The industry has more data than true insights. We don't need numbers, we need the intelligence to guide our investment opportunities." A great reminder from Brian Perkins, former VP-Corporate Affairs, Johnson & Johnson.

3. **Loyalty is a virtue:** I'll never forget the conversation I had with a prospective hospitality client who was ready to pull the trigger on a review. When I asked her for the rationale she simply stated, "They don't worry about my business the way I do and seem to be more interested in gaining new business." The first guideline in any new business plan is to keep your old business! How? By exemplifying sincere loyalty which in this business is absolutely a virtue.

So what happened after that closing argument in 1870? People present at the trial reported that when Counselor Vest finished his speech, there were few present in the courtroom, the jury included, whose eyes were dry. And the adage of a man's best friend was born that day. That single word that can sum up this unbreakable bond? Trust. Apply it to your client relationships too and see how man's best friend can help man's best business practices.

*Lisa Colantuono is Co-President of AAR Partners, a prominent agency search consultancy since 1980.*

**Place of first publication: LinkedIn, March 26, 2015**

## Can Improv Improve Marketing?

This article is by Lisa Colantuono, Co-President at AAR Partners.

Improvisation is a form of theater where most or all of what is performed is created in the moment. So how can the lessons of improv improve marketing? After participating in the Forbes CMO Excursion with the Wharton Future of Advertising Program, it was easy to see that improv is much more than just tickling a funny bone. Improv instructors teach their students how to be confident, collaborative, emotionally in tune, natural content creators and great listeners. Sound familiar? They're all also vital skills for successful marketers. The more they're practiced and honed, the more marketers will be innovative and effective in their roles as brand stewards.

There are more than a few lessons that can be borrowed from improv but the top three that stood out are the same three crucial needs highlighted in most marketing discussions today: listening, experimentation and inspiration.

**Listening.** How often is it said that listening skills are vital to career success? But how often do we actively listen instead of just waiting for our turn to speak? So often we're multi-tasking or "half-listening" during meetings and conversations that we not only miss much of what is said, but also (and more importantly) miss the opportunity to form a stronger connection to the person speaking. Research suggests that we only remember between 25% and 50% of what we hear. That's a startling statistic. In improv, as with business conversations, dialog isn't scripted. Improvisers must actively listen, focus, observe and be able to adapt and react quickly to what's being said. If a participant tunes out for a second, a critical detail may be missed and the scene will falter. Lesson learned? With the constant stream of communication being sent every day from a myriad of constituents, making a conscious effort to hear not only the words being said but, more important, understanding the complete message being sent is a crucial best practice.

**Experimentation.** Innovation is increasingly at the center of many marketers' agendas as the connected consumer continues to challenge and change brand interaction. Marketing principles haven't changed but the tactics have. According to John Costello, president and global marketing and innovation officer at Dunkin' Brands, "The danger is getting caught up in the tactics that we lose sight of why consumers should choose your brand." And innovation is the foundation of why consumers build relationships with certain brands over others (take note of Costello's title). Improv teaches us how to take risks and mine our imagination for new and previously unseen approaches. It offers the security that there is no right or wrong but rather a choice you make that you need to run with and support. It reminds us to forget what we know and reconstruct from the ground up in order to be truly creative and innovative. Experimentation breeds innovation by helping us to lose the fear of failure and instead knowing that failure is critical to learning and reaching new heights.

**Inspiration.** Many consumers today choose brands with an authentic higher-order purpose behind the brand and they wear those brands as a badge. This is particularly true for that huge – and elusive - Millennial market. Tom's Shoes, Juice

Press, Chipotle, Zappos are but a handful of the companies that embody this philosophy and for which consumers are proud to be brand advocates. They feel inspired and want to inspire others by sharing the story and inviting them to be part of the group. That's improv at the core. As improvisers, the participants are in it together, supportive of each other and inspiring the other actors to take the story to the next level. Improv is a team effort without leading roles. What's the correlation to the brand's marketing department? It's vital to remember that marketing is a collaborative team effort, which, in its most successful iteration, keeps the momentum going and the story strong in order to respond to daily consumer demand and hopefully, to gain their trust and loyalty and inspire their lives.

There is nothing stronger than developing new ideas through a collaborative, supportive, inspirational and non-judgmental team. There are no mistakes, only opportunities, "only beautiful, happy accidents." as Tina Fey, a master of improve, calls them. In improv, you can take any statement in any direction. Apply it to marketing and watch your innovation soar.

**Place of first publication: Forbes, December 1, 2014**

## Prospecting Needs To Be Treated Like NFL Footballs

Written by Lisa Colantuono | @aarlisa

Although Eli may have watched his brother play the toughest and most disappointing game of his life a couple of weeks ago, there is always next season for both of the quarterback brothers. As their dad, Archie Manning said at the end of the Super Bowl meltdown, "It's football." It may be football but there are some vital lessons to be learned for new business. For example, the number one lesson is strategy is everything, execution is king and nothing is simply left to chance.

Let's take the spotlight off Peyton and put the focus on the other brother here. What do Eli Manning's footballs have in common with the new business process? The football in his hands is familiar as an old friend and he rails against probability. The star quarterback has 12 to 20 footballs for each game that are meticulously groomed and prepped according to his specific needs and this football grooming process is months in the making. The footballs are brushed, scoured, primed, soaked using various apparent and semisecret procedures. The goal is to increase the chances that every pass Eli makes will connect with its intended receiver.

When it comes to new business, the same idea is relevant. Nothing should be left to chance. Being proactive instead of reactive to prospective business with rational reasons behind every outreach effort increases your chances of success. When you pick up the phone for a "cold call" it should be warm. How do you heat them up? Do your due diligence and research the prospective client's consumer needs, behaviors, purchasing journey; know their NPS and KPI figures; figure out where they stand in the category. We call this the three C's of prospecting: category, consumer and culture.

Category experience is typically considered a benefit but it can also work against you if dialed up too much. For example, when managing a health insurance review, the client was impressed with one of the semi-finalist agencies simply because the agency had deep experience with one of the marketer's competitors which the client team thought very highly of with regard to their brand positioning. On the other hand, when managing a QSR review, one of the semi-finalist agencies over-highlighted the fact that they had very deep experience with one of the client's primary competitors. The client team saw it as tunnel vision and eliminated that agency from the mix. When it comes to consumer experience, agencies simply can't have enough when it comes to prospecting and pitching. The more you know about the client's consumer, the better. Of course, that doesn't mean only demographics and psychographics. Behavioral insights, the decision-making process and purchasing journey are all vital to marketers. According to the CEO of the company, "It's all about experiential communication plans leading to engagement based on behavioral insights." Most of all know why and how your agency can complement the marketer's culture and uniquely help a particular brand which will increase the chances that your outreach will connect with the prospective client.

Of course, like Manning's footballs, this doesn't happen overnight. It takes prep time and sometimes weeks of data gathering and interpretation into core human insights. Clients can easily sniff out the "dialing for dollars" game and have no interest in entertaining the call. "I never answer my phone," says a CMO of a fast food chain. "I get nearly 200 cold calls a day and there's nothing specific to me!" In June 2013, I was invited to participate in the Forbes CMO Network and Wharton Future of Advertising Program CMO excursion, along with a group of 30 industry executives responsible for their corporate brands. I asked a handful of those executives two specific questions: "How many solicitation emails do you get on a monthly basis? Do you respond or even read the emails?" On average, these executives receive close to 1,500 unsolicited emails per month and the common answer to the second question was, "No, unless it is relevant and timely to my needs."

Timing! That idiom holds true: Being in the right place at the right time. It's just like the timing of a perfect pass from the New York Giants' star quarterback. But it is also about knowing what to do and say when you find yourself in that lucky spot. Once you have done your homework you still need to reach out with brand new information tailored to their needs but it must feel like it's been proven so the prospect isn't the guinea pig. "Don't just prospect me. Build a relationship by offering new insights about my brand, category or consumer and exemplify the success your agency has had with similar brands by offering your unique capabilities," says Aliza Perruzzi, Director of Marketing, Century 21 Department Store.

Or as Eli Manning says, "I want a brand new ball that feels like it is ten years old." The same applies in new business prospecting: offer new insights, tailored to the client's business with a unique point of view only your agency can offer based on weeks of prep time, have real rationale behind reaching out and leave nothing to chance. Leaving nothing to chance also means learning when to say no. Eli Manning turns down hundreds of footballs simply because they don't feel comfortable in his hands. The same should apply to agencies' new business process. Search and selection will always be a vital part of agency growth. But it's exhausting and costly to be ambulance-chasing instead of building relationships. Especially when you're missing relationships with marketers for whom you can offer specific benefits to help increase brand equity, market share and ROI. Let's face it, the number one concern for all marketers is obvious…accountability. According to the legendary John Hayes, CMO at AMEX, "Marketing must be more effective, creative and accountable."

Although the New York Giants wasn't a Cinderella team this year (and unfortunately, Eli's brother's team didn't prevail), it's still no wonder why star quarterbacks stand out from the pack. The same applies to luminary agencies with outstanding new business success rates in the industry.

**Place of first publication: Agency Post, March 3, 2014**

## CMOs, Shifting Brands From Nouns To Verbs Should Be A Key Marketing Goal

This article is by Lisa Colantuono, Co-Partner AAR Partners, an agency search consultancy.

I was privileged to participate in the 2013 Forbes CMO Summit in Miami along with almost 100 other marketing leaders from some of the world's biggest and most innovative companies. This year's summit focused on "The Transformational CMO: Marketer as Enterprise Value Creator."

"As data, analytics, technology and consumer behavior continue to take new forms, never has it been more important to learn and understand the varying engagement tactics that are being implemented effectively to reach consumers and drive bottom-line growth," said Bruce Rogers, chief insights officer and head of the CMO Practice at Forbes Media.

And technology was part of the summit from the moment delegates checked in at the hotel. Microsoft distributed the Nokia Lumia 920 phone to each attendee and placed an NFC (near field communication) tag on each attendee's badge. Why? So that delegates could instantly snag "digital business cards" with their smartphone at a short range instead of handing out the now-passé business card. It was another example of how the flood of data is at the point of being infinite. But the crux of the conference was about moving past myriad numbers to a true melding of science and art to craft a marketing strategy that is engaging.

One could safely argue that much of the deep data designed to develop core consumer insights becomes more of a hindrance than a help if it's not translated into a meaningful purpose that offers a benefit to the end user. That key purpose must be emphasized in a story that captures, informs and empowers consumers, eventually creating life-time brand advocates. According to Steve Wilhite, executive VP and CMO, Medidata Solutions, "My responsibility is to create a brand vision and inspire my agency, while they're responsible for human-centric, innovative ideas crafted into a well-written, engaging story with share-power." It's easy to see that having crucial data is supportive when it comes to storytelling, except when the continuous stream of real-time numbers leads to knee-jerk decisions."

"Infobesity" was the term used to describe the disease where the absorption of information is more than can be handled. But marketers are inquisitive people by nature, and they're interested in learning more as long as that "better mousetrap" is intriguing, innovative and relevant to their brand and consumers. "I'm not interested in seeing the constant stream of data every single day," said David Rosenthal, senior VP, Corn Refiners Association. "Instead, I want that core insight that's going to ignite my consumer."

After much conversation about the idea of the rapidly changing role of the CMO throughout a packed couple of days, it was agreed that the increasingly empowered and skeptical consumers have and are continuously changing demands on the marketplace. As a result, marketers must focus on five key areas, according to executive-search firm Spencer Stuart: Tighten brand purpose, experiment more, energize the organization, be courageous and grab hold of innovation.

Marketers need less quantity when it comes to numbers and more qualified intelligence to be innovative and guide their investment opportunities. After all, their role as a CMO is riding on it, and although the average tenure has increased from a low of 23 months in 2004 to a high of 45 months in 2012, according to Spencer Stuart, it is still a turbulent marketplace.

The common thread of advice over two days summed up in one sentence? Turn big data into engaging human insights in order to help brands become a verb instead of a noun in the marketplace.

**Place of first publication: Forbes, November 6, 2013**

## Human Experience: The New Media Channel

This article is by Lisa A. Colantuono, Co-Partner, AAR Partners, an agency search consultancy.

I was invited to participate in the Forbes CMO Network and Wharton Future of Advertising Program CMO Excursion on June 27, along with a group of 30 industry executives responsible for their corporate brands. The question that Wharton posed to its extended contributing committee prior to the CMO excursion was, "What could/should 'advertising' look like in 2020?" The points of view submitted from the committee were reviewed and presented to the attendees; the discussion focused on the new mindset for the future of advertising–"Advertising" 2020–around collaboration, continuous learning and "glocal" approaches.

After much conversation about the idea of "Advertising" 2020 and its implications on the CMO, it was agreed that increasingly empowered and skeptical consumers are continuously changing demands on the marketplace. Most important, per Wharton's research, these skeptics are:

- converging on personalization
- converging on communities
- converging on channels
- converging on choice
- converging on value

The marketers in the group shared more than three dozen challenges they face daily as a result of demands and expectations created by consumers. Top challenges: data explosion, social media, proliferation of channels, shifting demographics and, of course, making the brand relevant to the consumer in a crowded space.

Marketers must create human-centric brands that develop connections that truly count. Connections count by lifting burdens or reducing stress or adding some kind of ideals that the consumer values in their community.

So how does all this impact agencies? Communications plans must be data-driven, "tradigital", human-centric and agile, where the brand establishes a valued relationship with the consumer and earns the consumer's trust. Bottom line, consumers want to feel more in-control – a basic human desire – and therefore, have a meaningful association with the brand. After all, it's not about branding anymore–it's about "bonding."

Consumers are no longer buying brands. Instead they are investing in brands. That sense of trust so vital for a successful consumer-brand relationship? It's created through social *listening* that support real-time *solutions* that brands *uniquely* offer to them.

**Place of first publication: Forbes, July 3, 2013**

## Starting a new agency? Thoughts you should consider before turning the key in the door.

By: Lisa A. Colantuono, Co-Partner, AAR Partners, Co-Founder, Access Confidential.

Lots of new business advice from AAR Partners has been given over coffee throughout the years regarding a myriad of topics. But one topic manages to pop up over and over when industry executives decide to create a "break-away" agency. The question is often asked,

"What advice would you give to someone starting a new agency today?"

It's a loaded answer to a loaded question. However, there are a few vital points to keep in mind if you decide to give it a whirl today.

The **first piece of advice** starts by knowing about my 4 ½ -year old nephew who has been calling me on his mother's iPhone since he was 3 years old. Now at the ripe old age of 4 ½, he calls me on FaceTime while watching TV during breakfast while playing a game on his iPad. Welcome to the world of iBabies! *The point?* **Digitally-centric thinking is a must.** Many marketers appreciate mid-sized agencies today but still have a weak perception of their digital and social media capabilities.

"I'm very happy with the personalized service from our current mid-sized agency…feels like they are truly vested in my business but the digital and social media can be weak," says Ed, CMO of a QSR chain.

*Second bit of advice?* **Deep data.** Again, marketers seem to agree that those smaller and mid-sized agencies have less access to deep data. But here's the opportunity. The amount of data being streamed every day is overwhelming. In fact, it's useless unless you're filtering the right data at the right time and interpreting it properly for the right insights. The industry seems to have more data than true insight. **Marketers need fewer numbers and more intelligence to guide the investment opportunities.** According to Beth Comstock, CMO at General Electric,

"The future of marketing is combining an understanding of consumers' behavioral characteristics and data science."

**Last, but certainly not least, is the importance of talent.** Creative must be backed up with **strategic talent that stems from compelling research.** Hiring more people who have experience in all marketing disciplines will create much more comprehensive agency teams.

"Hire the best you can afford and then try to afford more – make sure you don't compromise even at the lowest levels," says Jill Ackerman, Director of Marketing Analysis and Research, Lindblad Expeditions.

Starting an agency is no easy task. Then again, anything worthwhile takes more than just some luck but hopefully, these few bits of advice will improve your chances of success.

Click on the following links to learn more about AAR Partners, a leading North America agency search consultancy and Access Confidential, a new business resource tool developed by new business people for new business people. Includes:

- Industry news alerts
- Analyst reports
- Search consultant insights
- Executive contact information
- Client-agency relationships
- Search history
- Executive profiles
- Advertising spending
- Creative sampling

**Place of first publication: Fuel Lines, July 9, 2013**

## Calling An Agency Review? Top Three Reasons Why The CMO Should Be Part Of The Process From The Start

This article is by Lisa Colantuono, Co-Partner of AAR Partners, an agency search consultancy.

Chemistry is vital but compatibility is the core of a successful relationship, and when relationships have both it sets the stage for enduring partnerships that create some case-study results. Yet the average tenure for many client-agency relationships range anywhere from four to six years. Why?

AAR Partners recently received a call from a spirits company inquiring about our service to manage a review. Whenever we receive these calls, our policy is to ask, "Why are you considering an agency search?" The intention behind the question is to evaluate if the search is truly necessary. In this case, the potential client responded, "It's five years. It's time." The hidden meaning behind that answer is usually one of relationship problems, change in client and/or agency leadership, poor results and/or quite often flat creative.

Just like in personal relationships, divorce has become commonplace in business relationships. The toll on lives in terms of behavioral and societal difficulties defy measurement, and when it comes to business break-ups, there is a deep economic impact for both sides. Aside from the lost income to the agency, the client also suffers a loss by needing to go through a learning curve with a new agency aside from the two to three months it typically takes to go through the process of a properly managed agency review.

So how do some client-agency relationships endure for two, three or even 10 times the industry average like, say, General Mills and Saatchi & Saatchi since 1928, or Wrigley and Energy BBDO since the 1933? They don't consider themselves "client-agency relationships." Instead, they consider themselves "friends all contributing to a successful business partnership." And it all starts with the CMO as the keystone of the friendship.

Here are the key characteristics of successful relationships and why CMOs must be part of a new agency relationship starting with the agency search:

**Friendship.** Strong friendships create staying power. In the business world, strong relationships create enduring partnerships. They not only enjoy rolling up their sleeves at the same conference room table, but also breaking bread together. So what does this have to do with the CMO being part of the review process from the start?

People like people who have similar personalities, work ethics and integrity. Of course, all are necessary for successful relationships but hard to determine if the CMO is not in the room. "Fit is everything. At the end of the day, your agency and CMO must have a deep personal connection that leads to transparency and trust. Their personalities and working styles have to not only be compatible, but also need to be perfectly aligned," according to Amy Muntz, president of Neiman.

**Communication.** As obvious as this may seem, constant communication is key to any successful relationship, whether it is personal or business, and it must be solid from the start. Those who are able to openly express their thoughts, insights, hesitations and concerns instead of burying frustrations always have a way of coming out at some ground-breaking position. Again, this starts with the CMO. The CMO who articulates the vision not only for the company but also for the brand is what separates the good CMOs from the great. If the CMO isn't part of the agency-review process from the start, there is a tremendous missed opportunity to ensure that everyone on both the client and agency side are on the same page. If not, that vision can be subject to interpretation and in danger of not being translated into transactions in the end.

There are often times when CMOs feel that they will empower their team to manage the review process and they will be part of the final pitch as an "objective third party." There is a lot of value behind leading but not micromanaging. However, we've come to realize that if you don't come to the first meeting, you should not go to the last. "In theory, it is great to give authority to the team who works on the day-to-day agency relationship, but sometimes those decisions are overturned later in the process by the CMO, therefore turning the process on its head, which can be demoralizing for the marketing and agency team," says Barbara Stefanis-Isreal, senior VP and director of marketing for MARC USA.

**Collaboration.** Great collaborative efforts come from great chemistry, and great chemistry must be determined from the start, which is why CMOs should be part of chemistry meetings scheduled at the start of the process. "Marketers are often quick to stress collaboration both from and within their agencies. Yet, they sometimes fail to collaborate within their own marketing departments," says Michael Palma, president of The Palma

Group. Chemistry meetings are a key opportunity to evaluate agency philosophy and culture, approach to business and creative solutions, as well as team dynamics within and between the client/agency teams. CMOs that arrive only for the final decision are in jeopardy of making a subjective decision based solely on creative instead of a comprehensive decision regarding the entire process based on research, strategic thinking, integrated business solutions and measurement. It also sets the tone for a non-collaborative relationship that's often the set-up for a short-lived agency relationship.

Client-agency teams must be in sync from the start, and that begins with having the CMO in the room. They set the stage, share the vision, define the role of the marketing team and establish expectations. Scott Goodson, chairman of StrawberryFrog, says, "CMOs should dig into the team and experience first-hand how they come up with strategic and creative excellence, how they think on their feet, how they react to change."

That sense of security so vital for both parties in the relationship? It's dependent on the CMO being part of the process from the start.

**Place of first publication: Forbes, September 19, 2012**

## Uniting the masses will help single you out!

By: Lisa Colantuono

There isn't an agency that meets with AAR Partners (a 30-year agency search consultancy in case you're unfamiliar with the name) that doesn't start or end with one of the following questions: "Who are the ad agencies that are doing things well today? What are successful agencies doing to crack the clutter? How do agencies attract clients' attention?"

The answers that are often given include setting strict objectives, developing pitch lists, determining goals and being extremely focused on categories or target markets where the agency has knee-deep experience. It's a start but they often produce ordinary results. Everyone is trying to crack the clutter and be the one standing out from the pack like a beacon in the night but going about the prospecting process by typically doing the same things and expecting different results. Of course, it's the definition of insanity too! So what are the answers to this age old question of successful prospecting?

The agencies that do seem to grasp marketers' attention are those that create bonds with consumers rather than just creating brands. Those purpose-driven brands that create attraction rather than just attention to themselves are the ones that marketers are most intrigued with and often want to know the agency talent that is behind that movement!

Long gone are the days of the monologue. In fact, the dialogue is also outdated. Today, communications is a "trialogue." Consumers must be able to interact with the brand physically, mentally, emotionally or viscerally allowing them to bond with the brand. Of course, one of the most impactful ways to contribute to the conversations and help create movements is through social media. Brand managers no longer control the conversation around the brand's image. Instead brands now earn the right to word of mouth since consumers are no longer willing to be subject to conventional messaging that speaks at them.

Instead they want to engage in authentic conversations through experiences that inform, entertain and empower. They're less interested in transactions and more impressed with connections that count. As a result, social media is today's necessity which is why major marketers such as Procter & Gamble, Dell, Converse, and Lexus are shifting more dollars towards social media. "Ninety percent of CIOs today are making their purchase decisions through social media," Karen Quintos, Dell CMO.

Zappos, Starbucks, Burt's Bees, JetBlue, Tom's Shoes...these are purpose-driven brands that attracted a mass following by going against conventional approaches, using "tradigital" media, creating emotional connections, and offering more than just a cup of coffee, a pair of shoes or a means of transportation. What about the agencies behind the creation of these cultural movements by forming a "need" to be part of the group and inviting the masses to bond with the brand? Those are the ones that stand out from the crowd and crack the clutter when prospecting new clients!

**Place of first publication: Uprising, January 25, 2012**

## Treat Your Clients Like Prospects and Vice Versa

By: Lisa Colantuono

When the Advertising Agency Register, originally a British import, opened its doors in 1980 to help marketers with the process of agency search and selection, there was an unspoken gentleman's rule: mega-agencies threw back the smallest fish – at that time it was usually accounts less than $5 million in billings.

Sometime in the past three decades, the "gentleman's rule" has vanished into thin air. Agencies have evolved to pitch everything and anything that presents itself as an opportunity, with the biggest shops sometimes pitching accounts and projects for far less money than they ever have.

It's a phenomenon no doubt fueled in part that last year marked the sharpest percentage decline in ad spending since the Great Depression, with the nation's top 100 advertisers cutting spending almost 8%, according to Kantar Media.

An environment with more shops willing to throw their hats in the ring can complicate marketers' search for the best new agency partner, often sucking up more time and expense for the client and, perhaps more problematically, for the agency.

The two primary avenues agencies use in the pursuit of new business are prospecting potential accounts and participation in agency reviews. But in both cases, clients are becoming frustrated with those who aren't doing sufficient homework or who aren't honest about the commitment their agency can make to the business.

In the case of prospecting, how should agencies go about finding qualitative leads? It's definitely not by "dialing for dollars." Agencies must evolve from the cold-calling mentality. A marketing executive at one of the most recognized brands in the world recently expressed to us his frustration on cold calling. "Don't waste your time calling me unless you do homework first," he said. "Understand my business, my industry, my consumer before you pick up the phone and explain how you can help me with my marketing issues and add value to my day."

There are four quadrants to think about when prospecting for new business, in the following order:

**Referrals.** We are in the business of relationships, and the people who trust you are the people who will offer positive word of mouth. Trust is the greatest competitive advantage.

**Agency capabilities.** If you're lacking in a particular area, strategically align your agency with one where you can complement each other.

**Buzz.** Be an expert in a particular area and let everyone know about the value of your expertise.

**Don't bombard.** Don't drop the mailings and the follow-up calls, but be smart and selective when doing them.

Many of the same rules for prospecting apply to participating in a client-led or search-consultant-led review. Agencies need to consider whether committing to responding to a request for proposal is something they really want or need to do. After all, to serve a client's business best, agencies have to blur the lines between their own business and that of the marketer's.

In a recent conversation, a hospitality-industry marketer summed up the rationale for considering a review in these words: "The agency is creatively strong but doesn't worry about my business the way I do!"

It brings to mind an old cliché that bears repeating: Treat your prospects like clients and your clients like prospects. If you don't, rest assured there is a long line of agencies showing your client how they can add value to the marketing-communications plans that your agency is neglecting. And it's your current clients, when serviced properly, who will become your best advocates and resource for organic growth.

The agency-client dynamic has changed during the past three decades, for better and worse. But some best practices should remain the same: Agencies must be honest with themselves about the level of commitment they can offer a new client; offer value-based solutions when reaching out to prospects; and focus on giving current clients the same attention they demonstrate to potential new partners.

**Place of first publication: AdvertisingAge, August 13, 2010**

## Cracking the Clutter! What Babies Can Teach Ad Agency New Business Executives About Prospecting

By: Lisa Colantuono

Many new business executives in the industry know that I'm in love with a two-and-a-half-foot, 26lb little guy…yes, my nephew. And if you want to see my little love, every Saturday I post a new photo of him on Facebook. So, besides getting a real workout once a week during my babysitting session with him, I realized he also exemplified how new business executives should think about prospecting. How? Let me explain.

There isn't an agency that meets with AAR Partners that doesn't start or end with the questions, "What are successful agencies doing to crack the clutter?" or "How do agencies attract clients' attention?" We often hear their answer is strictly setting objectives, developing pitch lists, determining goals and being extremely focused on categories or target markets where the agency has knee-deep experience. Don't get me wrong, there is nothing inaccurate with this approach but the value of exemplifying unexpected results is often forgotten!

Babies (like my favorite nephew) are captivated by the most unexpected results. Adults, on the other hand, focus on the outcomes that are the most relevant to their goals. They focus on objects and objectives that will be most useful to them. But babies play with objects that will teach them the most! The key…they draw on anything new, unexpected or informative.

At AAR Partners, we receive hundreds of letters, mailers,

emails, credential and collateral pieces that seem well…rather programmed, "more about me and less about you" and simply expected. The element of surprise (or the value of exemplifying unexpected results), isn't usually communicated. Agencies fall into the same pattern of churning out information about the agency and often forget to be informative. They forget to teach their prospect something of value.

Babies are captivated by unexpected results…just like CMOs! They need to see the value, something new or be surprised by unexpected results. They need to know that their brand is going to attract consumers by pulling them, rather than pushing them along. Crystallize how your agency has demonstrated unexpected and exceptional results for clients' business, make it relevant to the specific advertiser you're speaking to and in turn, captivate the prospect.

So, the next time you see a baby captivated by something unexpected (or informative), remember, that's the concept of how an agency could crack the clutter. And the results can be rewarding for everyone.

**Place of first publication: 4A's Business Development Blog, October 30, 2009**

# A Perfect Storm Warrants a Perfect Plan

By: Lisa Colantuono

In May 2005, analysts warned that oil could "super-spike" to $105 a barrel and economists were prophesying that the American economy as a whole might be sailing into choppy waters. Well, they are no longer prophecies. They are realities.

The fact is we've hit the perfect storm. The housing market is in total flux with mortgage debt ballooning from $4.9 trillion in 2001 to almost $10 trillion in 2007. The upheaval in the oil industry doesn't seem to be coming toward any kind of order. Instead, crude oil prices have hit record highs of around $147 a barrel earlier this summer. And the greater threat to American families than the rising prices of oil is the surging costs of groceries. Food costs are increasing at the fastest rate since 1990 with jumps anywhere from 20-60 percent.

As with energy, higher food costs cut into discretionary income that buys everything from cars to computers to movie tickets and drives the consumer-based U.S. economy. So where does that leave the advertising and marketing industry? FedEx Kinko's released the results of its national "Signs of the Times" small business survey last month.

Close to 100 percent of the small business owners polled were moderately to very concerned about the current economy's impact on their business. However, decreasing their marketing and advertising budgets is not a likely course of action. Instead, staying connected to customers – especially during taxing times –

is imperative. It is vital for businesses to remain visible.

The burning question we hear from lots of agencies during these turbulent times is, "How do we increase new business?" Let's start with the old adage of treating your clients like prospects and your prospects like clients. We are fighting a perfect storm and each agency needs to develop its own unique perfect plan to weather the storm.

Since each agency is distinctive, then each agency should have the perfect plan that best suits *them* and *their* offerings. It sounds so basic and we often see agencies nodding their heads and mumbling under their breath, "Well, of course. Communicate what is unique about us and how we can make a difference. I got it!" Although we're all in agreement, we often see the same things being done over and over again with the expectation of a different outcome. Yes, it's the definition of insanity. Having a crystal clear definition of who you are as an agency allows you to clearly communicate the unique value you can offer to a help solve a client's (current or prospective) problems. Gone are the days of "telling and selling," especially during the times when the signs of an imminent recession are all around us.

During one of AAR's New Biz IQ sessions, we helped an agency to crystallize not so much how they differ from their cluttered competitive landscape, but rather the *value* that *they* bring to solving marketing problems because in a tumultuous economy, there is a shift in attitude toward value orientation. And there is a lesson to be learned here. Emphasize core values during the economic downturn, starting with the value you bring through your relationships with your current clients. The mentality during these times is just like it is in the summer – the thought is everyone is on vacation, so don't make as many calls.

Similarly, the thought is everyone is not buying during a recession (even though we're not officially in a recession, we're close enough), so don't make the calls. Bottom line: The business goes to those who make the calls, starting with your own clients. Commit to learning. Those who think they know everything have nothing to learn. It's a great time to look at things from a fresh perspective. How can you do things better or different? Serve clients smarter?

We've heard it a number of times and it is well documented: Brands that don't constrict into a ball during bad economic times and increase their communications, while competitors are cutting back, can improve market share and return on investment at lower cost than during good economic times. Furthermore, doubtful consumers need the reassurance of familiar brands. In addition, more consumers are watching a screen at home, which can deliver higher than expected audiences at a lower cost.

Support your client by having an even deeper understanding of consumers and how they are redefining value and responding to the recession. Price elasticity curves are changing. Consumers take more time searching for durable goods, are more willing to postpone purchases, trade down, or simply buy less. The more you know about the consumer and how to build and strengthen brand relationships instead of making a transaction, the more valuable you're going to be to your client in the long term. In return, clients that are convinced of the significant impact your agency has made on their business will pay back twofold: It's a great way to grow organically and it will have a positive impact on word of mouth, which may bring in new clients for your agency.

Similar to the way your agency must emphasize core values by building stronger relationships with its current clients and, in turn, their consumers, the agency must also realize that it is the perfect time to start forging new relationships with marketers. And it may be in the agency's best interest to cast a wider net. The fact is the best time to introduce your agency to a prospect is when they are not looking for an agency. It takes the edge off of the entire introduction and no one is "selling" anything. However, you're doing something much more valuable; you're building trust, interest and the foundation of a potentially long-term relationship.

And when the economy is in the rebound stage, your efforts of exemplifying value, strengthening old relationships and building new ones will help your agency to thrive, rather than just survive a perfect storm.

**Place of first publication: Adweek, August 31, 2008**

# First, Do No Harm

By: Lisa Colantuono

There isn't an agency meeting that doesn't end with the question, "Who's hot?" It's an interesting question because the answer is contingent upon the "agency of the moment" and its winning streak. However, what that agency does to win new business isn't necessarily appropriate for another agency and its expertise.

So what is it that causes an agency to be sought out by clients? What are successful agencies doing to "crack the clutter"? Why is it that the client-agency relationships that endure far beyond the industry average of three-four years are few and far between?

Whether it's an increased track record of successful pitching, attracting more client business without pitching or having more enduring and successful client-agency relationships on the roster, there is only one solution. The answer is analogous to the Hippocratic oath taken by a physician: "First, do no harm." This is at the heart of the thinking of most successful services. They believe their success will come from taking care of their clients and helping them to become successful. The question that should be asked continuously is, "How can we help them succeed?" rather than, "What can we do to win the business?"

The command-and-control approach is over for the marketer, and for the agency trying to win business. Agencies that are engaging (not disruptive) and offering missing opportunities crack the cluttered agency environment and ultimately make a difference for the advertiser. Gone are the days of intrusion-driven communications. During a conversation with a potential client, the CMO pointed to a corner of his office piled with paraphernalia from agencies trying to grab his attention and stated, "What a waste of my space and their money!" As part of a review process, it's the agency that illustrates its deep interest in the advertiser's offering and sincerely wants to help the client that pulls ahead of the pack.

During a review for a restaurant chain, there was one agency that visited almost every restaurant in its region. The proposed account group spent days waiting tables and engaging patrons in order to understand the consumer and the opportunities and/or challenges faced from the inside. They truly wanted to figure out how to help the advertiser succeed.

We've all experienced the thrill and excitement of winning a new account. The key is to keep that exhilaration alive for many years, transcending the tough times and fueling itself on the good times. Onboarding workshops for client-agency newlyweds not only ease the transition into a new relationship, but also make it more effective faster and, ultimately, more enduring. It's not enough anymore to listen and learn. There's an acute need to act and make an impact.

In a recent onboarding workshop that AAR Partners conducted, the top attributes expected of each team all fell under the realm of "partnership." Some of the specific attributes clients expected of agencies were: proactively thinking about my business; quick to respond to my problems; and a dedicated team committed to my business. Some of the top attributes that agencies expected of clients were: sharing objectives; honest communication; and responsive and constructive criticism.

It's the agency that has the keen ability to guide a client in an engaging manner through an open and honest conversation that brings awareness and clarity to the marketing problem. Doing so promotes success for both parties.

This past November we attended the second annual industry dinner honoring "Enduring Relationships," presented by the Advertising Club and district two of the American Advertising Federation. How many relationships are celebrated each year, you ask? Five! Five out of thousands of relationships have endured beyond three decades and been celebrated each year. That begs the question: Can the committee continue to find 30-plus-year relationships, year after year, for an annual celebration?

So how do some client-agency relationships endure for two, three or 10 decades? The answer is simple, but the dedication needed to support it is much more demanding. The "enduring relationships" celebrated didn't consider themselves "client-agency relationships." In fact, that description was felt to be almost insulting to the celebrated teams. Instead, they considered themselves "friends all contributing to a successful business partnership."

The fact is we know that clients are looking for two assets from an advertising agency. They want a solid creative idea, which is the currency of advertising, and, equally important, they want the confidence that the agency will always ask the question, "What would I do if it were my business?"

**Place of first publication: Adweek, April 28, 2008**

## Chemistry is More Than Just an Attraction!

By: Lisa Colantuono

There is not a single agency meeting that AAR Partners finishes without hearing this question: "What are the most important criteria in winning a review?" After being involved in a myriad of agency pitches as the search consultant, there is a simple answer to a not so simple question. Chemistry! The review begins and ends on chemistry and all the demanding work in between is extremely vital!

But chemistry is not simply about 'love at first sight!' It is a step-by-step process. It is a process of building trust and effective communication. Yes, 'effective' communication. There is a difference between speaking the minutia of daily activities and having in depth discussions with the client as a true partner about the 'big picture' regarding their business needs. But I digress. As I said, chemistry is much more than skin deep. Is your agency truly interested in their product offering? What about your agency's interest level in their marketing issues or opportunities? Would you want to buy or use their product as a consumer? Is the agency willing to go as far as risking compensation based on its performance?

We often hear from an agency, "We're open in 'x' category, "so don't forget about us when you do a review for a company in 'x' category." Sure, we keep all those requests in mind, but we also find ourselves asking the same question. "Do you want just any 'x' account in that category on your agency roster or would your agency team like to work on a specific 'x' account?" It's definite that a client sees right through the agency that is pitching a 'category' rather than a specific 'brand.' For instance, when AAR managed the Ben & Jerry's review, we had a chemistry meeting with an agency that made the statement, "We need you on our roster." At that moment, the meeting was over. You could literally read the client's mind. "Do you need our business for your self-serving purposes or do you want to work with us on our business needs!"

There is one thing for sure: the client wants sincere interest, enthusiasm, as well as talent and smarts....and chemistry should encompass all of these. But chemistry is also about going the extra mile and is certainly in the details. AAR recently visited a number of agencies with our client for chemistry meetings. Selecting the finalists was a grueling process and extremely difficult 2-hour decision. It was not only those agencies that exemplified some smarts about their business, but also showed enthusiasm throughout the entire presentation that were selected to move forward in the review process. These agencies demonstrated that they had the entire agency behind the meeting and not just those people in the conference room. Those were the agencies that were selected to move forward as finalists. For example, at one meeting the entire agency applauded when the client entered the building to welcome them. No, we're not suggesting a 'stunt show' but there are certain simple chemistry building techniques that run deep. If you're pitching a fast food chain... yes, we think you should go flip burgers for a day. "Taste-test" the product! But exemplifying enthusiasm and chemistry can be as simple as writing a thank you note. Last year a hair splitting decision on agency finalists came down to a thank you note! The note exemplified true interest in the client's business and an appreciation for their time. To put it simply, our belief is that after an agency meeting the client should feel that, "The agency will think about my business as if it were their own!"

All of us know that there is no cookie-cutter approach to winning new business. But there are a number of questions an agency should ask itself if it is considering prospecting a new piece of business: Does our agency really want to work with this company or on this particular brand? Why? Is our agency ready to be flexible to the needs of this brand's specific business problems in order to resolve them? Does this opportunity of working on this business leverage what we are as an agency, what we know as an agency and more importantly, can we use that knowledge for the client in order to have a meaningful impact on their business?

Bottom line is this: Do your homework but also be true to yourself. If more agencies prospected clients' businesses that they were truly interested in, knew they could make a difference and did not pretend to be something they're not...the tenure of client-agency relationships would dramatically increase. And remember, Chemistry is key!

Happy prospecting!

**Place of first publication: TalentZoo, January 2008**

# CLOSING THOUGHTS

**@AARLisa: If you never failed, you didn't try anything new!**

The extraordinary comes out of facing the F-word in life. No, not that "F-word" – the other one. F-A-I-L-U-R-E.

Most rail against it and many live by the line, "Failure is not an option." We're taught from the time we reach elementary school not to fail tests or we won't get into honors classes, and if we don't take advanced classes, we won't get into a good college, and if we're not accepted into a prestigious university, we won't end up with a high-paying job, and without a job that pays well, we'll live a life of mediocrity. We learn to *fear* failure.

What we miss is the fact that failure can be amazing if we embrace it the right way. Bill Gates' first company, Traf-O-Data, failed miserably. Stephen King's first novel was rejected 30 times. The world of Disney would never have been created if Walt wasn't fired from a newspaper for having "no original ideas." If it weren't for Thomas Edison, we'd still be sitting in the dark, but he failed 1,000 times before creating the light bulb.

So what's the lesson? I'm not suggesting going out into the world and deliberately failing at what you set out to accomplish. However, failure can be the most valuable teacher we ever meet in our lives. We triumph most from mistakes as long as we are not overcome by failure, but instead overcome failure with fine-tuning. It's called the School of Hard Knocks for a reason, but those who succeed realize that *failure* is nothing more than the First Attempt In Learning, Understanding, Realizing and Executing.

There is no doubt that failure can be extremely frustrating regardless of whether it involves test taking, pitching multi-million dollar pieces of business or playing video games. When my nephew was four, he and I were playing a video game on an iPhone. I said to him, "This game is annoying." He asked me, "What's annoying?" I explained that the game was frustrating and that I kept losing. The advice from the little guy was simple: "Aunt Lisa, take your time and don't give up!"

In my office hangs a 20" x 24" framed reminder:

When things go wrong, as they sometimes will,
When the road you're trudging seems all uphill,
When the funds are low and the debts are high,
And you want to smile, but you have to sigh,
When care is pressing you down a bit,
Rest, if you must, but don't you quit.
Success is failure turned inside out—
The silver tint of the clouds of doubt,
And you never can tell how close you are,
It may be near when it seems so far,
So stick to the fight when you're hardest hit—
It's when things seem worst that you mustn't quit.
- Author unknown

As an agency search consultant in the ad world, I've had the privilege of attending many great pitch presentations and also the misfortune of witnessing many that spiraled south quickly. After much deliberation on why some pitches implode, I've found there are many potential explanations but the one that seems to stand out most, which has been said in various ways by numerous marketers, is: "The agency played it safe...there's nothing new and they didn't push me to feel uncomfortable enough to want more."

No one became successful by doing average work. No one has ever been recognized by doing work that's good enough. No one has ever left their mark on this world without putting their heart and soul into something that they believed would change the status quo for the better.

Don't be afraid to take a risk, but be sure to take intelligent risks. Learn from the failures of others. Learn from your own mistakes. Don't allow failure to be a verdict but instead an opportunity to do better. Fumbles pave the way for inspiration and creativity, which are the backbone of the advertising business.

I hope this little "nuggets of knowledge" book left you with insights, practical advice, and lessons from other people's stumbles and successes in order to help you prospect, pitch and steward more efficiently, effectively and successfully. Of course...a little luck never hurts either.

# THANK YOU & ACKNOWLEDGEMENTS

*"Strange, isn't it? Each man's life touches so many other lives.*
*When he isn't around he leaves an awful hole, doesn't he?"*
Clarence Odbody, *It's a Wonderful Life.*

There are many people who have gone in and out of my life.
Some have made a mark, others have left a footprint on my heart
and few have left an impression in my life forever…without them
there would have been an awful hole.

I am grateful for the countless people who have mentored me,
encouraged me and believed in me throughout the years.

To my mother and father: without either of you, I would not be
part of this universe helping to touch the lives of others and leave
it a better place.

My brother and sister-in-law: you have given me the two greatest
gifts anyone could ever want in life. Thank you for making me
"Aunt Lisa."

Tia Weil: you were one of my first true mentors to prepare me for
my professional life. I've tried to express how your inspiration and
friendship have impacted me over the years – but to no avail.

NYIT: thank you for trusting me to teach dozens and dozens of
students over the past 16 years as an adjunct advertising professor.
I'm honored to have been able to touch the lives of many students
entering the advertising industry.

The list of industry friends who have contributed to my career and knowledge of new business includes Laurel Rossi, Dean Buresh, Barb Stefanis-Israel, Donna Wiederkehr, Morgan Shorey, Kim Hunt, Gregg Wasiak, Lou Rubin, Sally Kennedy and many more – thank you so much.

To the countless clients who have trusted me to manage their agency reviews over the years: without you, I would not have flourished into the experienced new business consultant I am today enabling me to share my insights written here in this book.

To my Access Confidential team: without you, there would be no full-service new business center helping agencies to "prospect smAARt and avoid the pitch!"

Debra Wurzel, who is so talented at getting into my head and editing my words to create more impact than I could have imagined…you've taught me how to tighten it up and get to the core idea (or think in "Tweet-like" sentences). Much appreciated.

Last but certainly not least: Leslie Winthrop. You started as my boss and quickly developed into my business partner, but what I'm most grateful for is your friendship for the past 15 years. You've treated me like a daughter from day one and trusted me as your business partner as we founded and created an entirely new company together over the past decade. The days are long, but the years are short. Thank you with all my heart for being a part of my professional path, the tears from laughter and the crazy travel adventures. I look forward to the coming years as your *business* partner and especially as, your friend.

Most of all, I am grateful to GOD, who has created and blessed me with more gifts than I could ever pray for in a lifetime. For without HIM, I am no one.

## @AARLisa is a Member of the Following Twitter Lists:

Marketing Dot added by Ellen Curtis

Market Research added by Kantar Worldpanel

Advertising and Marketing added by Steve Koch

BOLO 2015 added by Nick Sargent

best00 added by Womanfruit

Hub Spotters added by Stefan Price

New Business & Sales added by Christian Banach

Marketing Mentor Friends added by Ilise Benun

AdAge Small Agency Confer added by Chas Porter

Super Startups added by Network Arte

BOLO 2015 Speakers added by BOLO AZ

Creative added by Alex

BOLO 2015 added by Scott Cowley

Design, Tech & Comms added by Sundee

How Design Live added by Carey Mercier

Industry Thought Leaders added by Inmotionow

HOW Speakers 2015 added by Tess Perez

ANA Masters 2014 added by Robert Moore and Jeffrey Hayzlett

Marketing added by Kasi Martin

Thought Leaders added by RSW/US and Lee McKnight Jr.

Advertising-and-Marketing added by Jason Kirk

NewBusiness added by Tedismert

Time to Go Viral added by Invierno en Lunas

The New Yorker added by Jeff Faria

Super Bowl Ad Tweet Meet added by Wharton FoA Program

ad industry added by West Herford

agencies added by West Herford

business intelligence added by Michael Rosenfeld

Gente mas lista que yo added by Gustavo Entrala

Marketing added by Diana Bald and Liz Arreaga

Helpers & Advisors added by John Young

Brands and Media Firms added by John Swagga

Many of the "little lessons" detailed in this book are the foundation of Access Confidential. I'm delighted to say that the Access Confidential team has proudly supported agency growth over the past decade and would be delighted to help you too…

Powered by AAR Partners, Access Confidential is the only comprehensive new business data, insights and service center developed by new business people for new business people to help agencies "prospect smAARt and avoid the pitch!"

"Thanks to Access Confidential, Moosylvania has won $3MM for less than a $12K investment over the past three years."
– Norty Cohen, Moosylvania Marketing

"It's a great tool that's a default stop for my entire team to supplement our secret sources of information. Well done Lisa and Leslie!" – Matt Weiss, Havas Worldwide

"Access Confidential is an amazing resource. In the world of new business, it is always hard to stay ahead of the game, but with Access Confidential I am able to stay up to date on everything including potential leads, executive movements, and what is going on in the market place. The first thing I recommend to anyone in the agency world is Access Confidential – if you don't have it, you should get it as soon as possible."
– Mike Ridley, the community

"I just wanted to send you a shout out and kudos on the WONDERFUL Access Confidential. I've been utilizing it extensively as well as relying heavily on your team. My research would be much less efficient without you guys!!"
– Ann Baxter, McCann Minneapolis

19884049R00146

Made in the USA
Middletown, DE
08 December 2018